LLOYD OF THE DANCE
MY LIFE

BY

LLOYD WRIGHT

To John + Tou × Magda × Castle Cheers By Lloyd

Published by New Generation Publishing in 2021

Copyright © Lloyd Wright 2021

First Edition

The author asserts the moral right under the Copyright, Designs and Patents Act 1988 to be identified as the author of this work.

All Rights reserved. No part of this publication may be reproduced, stored in a retrieval system or transmitted, in any form or by any means without the prior consent of the author, nor be otherwise circulated in any form of binding or cover other than that which it is published and without a similar condition being imposed on the subsequent purchaser.

ISBN 978-1-80031-221-0

www.newgeneration-publishing.com

New Generation Publishing

Dedication

To my loving and caring mother.
You will always be in my thoughts.
You are my light, my world.
You always made me feel I was your dearest son.

Acknowledgements

During my life I have met many wonderful people, and I would like to take this opportunity to thank them for their support and kindness. Firstly to my publisher, my family, my kids and grandkids, my personal nurse Lindsey Tuckwell, my next door neighbour Roy, Nicky and her mum and dad, my best buddy and like a brother to me (Norm), Mark Gorman, Simon Gray, Lee Kendall, Peter the Bear, Paul Dockram, Richard Whittaker, Gary Frankish, Paul B, my lawyer, Heather Howe, Gables mental health team (John, Sophia, Nikki), HMP Bullingdon library staff (Alison, Dawn, plus Sarah from the reading group), the Alpha course and all the volunteers, and Susan the American lady, the vicar at Bullingdon, the vicar at Stocken, the vicar at Ford, healthcare at Bullingdon, healthcare at Stocken, Wendy from the church in HMP, Ford healthcare at Ford, Psychiatrist at Ford.

CHAPTER ONE

I was born on 27th April 1976, in a leafy Hertfordshire town called Hemel Hempstead. The year I was born was one of the hottest years on record.

Hemel Hempstead is very close to Watford and is north up the M1 from London. One of its landmarks is the Plough roundabout, which is also known as the Magic Roundabout. The middle part is the largest one, with five smaller ones branching off from it. The location is also memorable for its former Kodak Tower, which was where the photographic film for cameras was made. Back in the 1970s, the area was popular with Londoners who wanted a more peaceful life.

My parents were one of the many families who saw the benefits of leaving London. My mother and father were both born and bred in London and they grew up in hard times after the Second World War. I have an older brother who is two years my senior, but we were not close as youngsters, and remain the same as adults.

Pauline Wright was my beloved mother, who did her best for her family all her life. Nothing was too much for her, and she worked hard to get us everything we needed. She came from a very big family. She had two brothers and four sisters.

My father's name was Steve Wright. I am not too sure about his side of the family as he wasn't very forthcoming about his earlier life. I do remember going to see his mum and dad who were my nan and grandad, only a few times, but I never visited any other relatives of his, if there were any.

My father was a very hard man and we often got the brunt of his anger. I can remember my brother and I getting a few beatings now and then for petty misdemeanours, and on some occasions for absolutely nothing at all, other than we were in the wrong place at the wrong time, when he wasn't in the mood to tolerate us. Despite this, he worked hard to put a roof over our heads, clothes on our backs and food on the table.

I always used to remember people joking when I was growing up, and saying that my dad, Steve Wright, was on in the afternoon on Capital FM Radio. This was because he had the same name as a popular DJ at that time. I was very familiar with his name, as my mother would always listen to him playing the Top 40s on the radio. The fact that they likened my dad to a radio DJ was an amusing thought, as I couldn't have thought of a more unlikely profession for him.

In fact, my father worked at an oil refinery for BP. He was an oil tanker driver, at the Hemel Hempstead Branch at Buncefield Lane, fuel depot. It was a massive area just off the M25, which held huge cylinders of oil and massive drums of petrol. My father's job was to fill a tanker up with fuel a few times a day and deliver it to petrol stations up and down the country, for people to fill up their cars. I recall him moaning to my mum, saying that he was sure that where he worked would one day blow up.

Little did he know that his words would come true. A few years later in 2005 there was a huge explosion, and people for miles around felt the vibrations of the blast. It caused so much devastation to everything in close proximity. Windows were shattered and car alarms set off. They had to close the entire industrial area off, and the smoke and fumes were going for miles into the sky.

Family friends who lived right next to the depot were unfortunate enough, to have their bungalow caught in the explosion. Simon, one of the eldest sons who lived there, was luckily working at home that day. His elderly mother was in the bungalow and if he had not been there to get her out, she might have lost her life.

He was outside in the yard working, when the explosion happened, and without any hesitation, and no thought for his own safety, he raced back inside the home which had become a fireball, to bring his mother out of there. He ushered her inside his Jeep and drove away as fast as he could. Just as he was doing this, the whole place just blew sky high. They were both very lucky I am pleased to say.

At the time when all of this was going on, I was on a flight coming back from Malaga to visit my kids that weekend. I was supposed to land at nearby Luton Airport, but they had closed it down because of the smoke billowing out of the depot. Out of the window of the aeroplane, I could see clearly what had happened, as we were diverted to Stansted Airport. Up until then, I had always taken my dad's complaints about the place blowing up as him being a bit dramatic, but he obviously knew what he was talking about.

My mum didn't work but stayed at home to look after my elder brother and I, and she was devoted to us. We never wanted for anything, and she was very loving and caring, and made sure we had everything.

What I didn't know was that before I was born when my mum was giving birth to my brother, she had a terrible time giving birth to him. He was a healthy baby boy when he was born, but my mum lost a lot of blood afterwards.

Years later when we were older, she used to tell us about it, and she believed that she had died that day when she was giving birth. She had some vague memories of nurses behaving strangely around her, as she was insistent that she had died, due to the amount of blood she lost. She always believed there was a bit of a cover up, because they dismissed her claims of dying. Regardless of this, she always maintained that they had made a mistake while trying to save her, and were covering themselves, as she clearly remembered having an out of body experience.

After what happened, she just wanted to be out of the hospital and home with my brother. She was relieved that the pair of them were still alive, and she didn't want to be in a place where she believed mistakes had been made, and not admitted to. My dad said she should have pushed for an inquiry about what really did happen that day, but Mum was just glad it was all over, and she was safely back at home. Since that day and for the rest of her life, she was understandably terrified of doctors and hospitals.

As it turned out, she had every right to be concerned, but she didn't discover the truth about that hospital, until years later. Despite her misgivings she returned to the same hospital to give birth to me. Although she was nervous upon her return, she was pleased to see that everything seemed to be under control, and she hoped that this time, nothing would go wrong. All the hospital staff seemed to know what they were doing, and neither she nor I were in any kind of distress. She made it out of the hospital grounds with both of us still in one piece, and with nothing untoward happening to either of us, but sadly this was not to be her last hospital visit.

It was over 20 years after my brother's birth that her suspicions about the wrongdoings of the hospital staff were confirmed.

My mum had a habit of using the laundrette, even though she had a washing machine at home. She liked the social aspect of it all. She would sit and chat to her friends, and also make lots of new friends there. She would often while away a few hours with them, chatting about the local community, and other general chit chat. She was well known in the community and she would help anybody if she could. Because of her friendliness, we were well known as a family.

On one particular day, she went to the assistance of a woman, who wasn't sure how to operate the machine. As she was showing her how to use it, they struck up a conversation. It started off as an everyday conversation, but when proper introductions were made, my mum was in for a big shock.

My mum had no idea that she was about to be told something which would bring back memories of an incident over 20 years earlier! The woman mentioned her sons, and in turn my mum told her that she had two sons, and it turned out that me and my brother were quite close to her sons in age. My mum remarked that the children might know one another, as they lived in the same area, and she casually mentioned the names of me and my brother.

The woman froze, and her face went pale.

She was silent for several minutes, and when she began speaking again, she spoke very quietly. She knew my mum's name was Pauline, as she had introduced herself at the beginning of their conversation, but now the woman knew our full names as well.

With the shock evident in her voice, the woman said, 'Oh my God, you said that your name was Pauline Wright. I've only just realised that we've met before, and in very unpleasant circumstances.'

Mum was understandably alarmed, by what this stranger was saying, and her worries were not eased, when the woman said, 'I'm so sorry, I have something to tell you. Let's go and get a cup of tea.'

Mum simply nodded silently, too concerned to do anything else. She couldn't even begin to imagine what this woman she'd only just met might have to say.

After they got their drinks, the woman took a few sips, before speaking again. It was clear she was very uncomfortable.

'Pauline, I was there at the birth of your first son. I was a nurse working at St Paul's Hospital that day.' For a few moments again she was quiet, then she continued, 'We lost you that day. You died and we resuscitated you!'

My mum was in bits as it brought back the memories of that day. However, her main feeling was one of relief to know that she hadn't been imagining things, as the hospital staff had led her to believe. She knew she had died that day and finally, finally, she had somebody confirming this for her.

The woman said she wasn't there the entire time, but when the alarm went off, she was in the room, and saw them bringing her back to life. She agreed with my mum that they must have done something wrong that day, as everything about the incident had been hushed up, and wasn't spoken about at the hospital.

My mum shrugged her shoulders, and explained, that she was lucky to be alive, and had simply been glad to get out of the hospital when it was all over. She told the woman, that she had not taken it any further all those years before.

Just like my dad, the woman said that she should have pushed for an inquiry. She added that she did understand that after what she had gone through at the time, the rigmarole of an inquiry would have been too much.

My mum was shaken for days after the conversation. She couldn't stop thinking about what the woman had told her. For over two decades, she had firmly believed that she'd had an out of body experience, and she had been made to feel that it was just her imagination when she mentioned it at the hospital. And when I was being born, she was overwhelmed with worry, after her previous experience at the hospital, but luckily everything went smoothly. Both my mum and I seemed to come out of the entire experience completely unscathed, or at least that's what she believed at the time.

It wasn't long before she realised that she had gone into that hospital again, and had come out with many years of worry ahead, but for different reasons this time.

When I was nine months old, the hospital discovered that I had been born with a disability, which only came to their attention as I began to develop. It's a congenital problem which causes the chest wall to grow inwards and squash the lungs and heart. This can lead to heart and breathing problems, and in some cases, it can be fatal if the inward growth continues.

Since it is difficult to predict how bad it will get, all that can be done is regular checks to monitor the situation, and an operation if it appears to be getting worse. Every six months I was taken to see a specialist at Harefield Hospital.

This constant monitoring only worsened my mum's worry, but she would always remain outwardly calm to reassure me.

As I grew older and understood more about my condition, my mum would always tell me that I was born an extra special baby. This helped to comfort me, and make the hospital visits a little more bearable.

CHAPTER TWO

We lived in a green belt area in a nice semi-detached house in a cul-de-sac. Our lives were fairly happy, as both our parents did all they could for me and my brother. The only problem was that my dad had a bad temper and could quite easily lose it. Often me and my brother would get a smack off him.

It all came to a head one day, when Mum saw that he was about to smack us, and she stood in front of him. She protected us, but was unable to protect herself, as Dad turned on her and hit her instead.

She was a good woman who would put up with a lot, but being knocked about wasn't ever going to be something she would tolerate. Immediately afterwards, she began divorce proceedings, and there was no turning back for her.

I was about 5 years old at the time my dad left us, but Mum always gave us a choice to see him, as she thought it was only fair. Me and my brother made our own choices about that and decided not to see him because we resented him after seeing him hit our mum.

The times we saw him were few and far between, and eventually fizzled out altogether. After that he didn't seem interested and we never met again. My mum was awarded the house as part of the divorce proceedings, so at least we had a roof over our heads.

From the age of 6 years old, I never received a birthday card or Christmas card from my dad, and he made no effort to contact Mum to arrange to see me and my brother. It was as though we no longer existed to him. Mum was left to look after the two of us and the house without any help. It was hard for my mum as a single parent, with two young boys to feed and look after, as well as paying all the normal bills, but she wasn't about to let the situation beat her.

Even though she had not had to work when she lived with my dad, she began to take on a number of different jobs, and also took in a lodger to make ends meet. She was an absolute star, and never complained about what a struggle it was. She just got on with it and did whatever it took, to make our lives good and to provide.

As we grew up, she made sure that we had all the latest clothes, and we never had to look at the things other kids had, and feel envious, because she would always find the money to get us what we wanted. We played in the streets a lot, and she bought us the bikes that were popular back then. The Chopper bike, with the 3-speed gear level in the middle, came first, then the Grifter, and later racers and mountain bikes.

When it came to the computers that all the kids were using back then, she somehow managed to buy each one for us as they became popular. We had the Atari, the Commodore and the Spectrum Sinclair. Inside our house, we had all the gadgets that everybody else had, such as the Beta Max recorder, and then VHS.

I remember one day watching the newly released 1982 video, *Thriller* by Michael Jackson on VHS, and jumping and dancing like a zombie in the front room. I was able to enjoy all of these things thanks to my mum. She was a top mother, and I was proud to call her Mum.

One thing we didn't go short of was holidays, as we used to go on camping holidays a lot when we were young. From the regular trips we took, I developed a real love of the outdoor life, and going on holiday, which remains with me to this day. Mum took us to the Isle of Wight, Wales, the Lake District and to France and Spain and travelling is still one of my favourite things.

Despite living as a single parent family, we were happy, and the only cause for concern back then was that my disability was getting worse. I regularly saw my local doctor for check-ups, and still attended six monthly appointments at Harefield Hospital with the specialist. I wasn't in any pain, although I did get breathless often. Even so, I was shocked when I was told that the inward growth of my chest was starting to crush my lungs and my heart. I had always been aware that this could happen, but I chose to put it to the back of my mind, so that I could try to lead a normal life.

The specialist at Harefield hospital, advised my mum to let me have an operation, which would help solve the problem. He explained that if I didn't have the operation sooner rather than later, it would become a much bigger problem as I got older. That might have been the ideal solution, except that Mum was advised that I might not come through the operation, as it was a major one with a lot of risk. And afterwards, it would be a long process to recover, with the timescale being years rather than months. So, on the positive side, if all went well like it should, I would be fine after the recovery, and would have no more problems with the condition as I grew up. The negative side was much more frightening, because even though I was only 6 years old, I understood that I might die in the process of having the operation. This was in the 1980s, and even though they had plenty of technology to work with, it certainly wasn't as efficient as things are nowadays.

The specialist could see that my mum was uncertain about what to do, so he suggested that she should go home and have a think about it. He told her to ring him the following week to let him know her decision. This was the worst possible situation my mum could have been put into. She didn't like hospitals because of what she had gone through herself. She wanted me to lead a full and healthy life, but the nagging doubt about the fact that I might not make it through the operation terrified her.

As young as I was, I could see she was hurting for me. We were very close, and my condition made us even closer. I loved her so much. She was an amazing mum, and all I wanted was for her not to have to worry constantly. During that week leading up to giving the specialist a decision,

Mum spoiled me rotten. We talked about it when I wanted to, and she would leave the subject alone if I seemed like I didn't want to talk about it.

She told me that she was going to leave the decision to me, because she didn't feel she could make such a life changing choice for me. She could tell I was scared, and she gave me so much comfort and love and reassurance. Before we knew it, the week had passed, but even then, she didn't pressure me. She simply told me that she would ask the specialist to give her longer to decide, if I wanted her to. In the end, I realised that there was no point in delaying, and I made the decision to go ahead with the operation. I wanted to be running around with my mates when I got older, not gasping for breath and possibly in a lot of pain.

It was a massive decision, and I was beyond terrified, but my mum made the call and they set a date for two weeks later. It seemed to drag by at first, but the last couple of days zoomed by. Next minute I was nil by mouth and lying in the hospital bed, and that was when it hit me. My mum had given her consent and signed all the correct paperwork. I was due to have the operation early the next morning. It was getting late and my mum couldn't stay the night as she had to get back for my brother. We cried together, and she gave me loads of love and hugs, and said she would be back first thing in the morning, before I went down for the operation. I was brave, and said, 'Okay Mum, goodnight. See you in the morning. Love you.'

My mum had only left the hospital an hour before. It was about 10pm and I couldn't sleep, I was so scared and worried I might die, and never see my mum again. My mind went back and forth over the benefits of having the operation, and then over the drawbacks, if I did have it or if I didn't have it.

Thinking back, I realise that it was too much for any 6-year-old to deal with, but in that moment, I made up my mind that I was going to go home to my mum. I jumped out of my bed ready to make my escape. The thing was it was late at night, and I was only 6 years old, and the decision had already been made, with all the paper signed.

I guessed if anyone saw me making a run for it, I would be in big trouble, but this didn't stop me. I couldn't call the nurse and tell her I was leaving, because I knew she wouldn't take any notice of me, so I decided I would just sneak off without telling anybody.

Shaking with fear that I might be dragged back to bed and forced to have the operation, I sneaked by a few other patients in their beds and past some nurses, then out into the corridor and down some stairs, and made it outside. YES!

I was running away still dressed in my white hospital gown, and it was so dark outside that it made me even more frightened.

I spotted a little patch of woodland and ran towards it to hide. When I got there, it was full of roses and stinging nettles, and I was scratched and stung. My arms were bleeding from the rose scratches and had bumps from the stinging nettles, and I was shivering from the cold and scared and worried. I was in a right mess.

I guessed it wouldn't be long before they noticed that I wasn't in my bed, and then there would be panic stations. I soon realised that I was right, as the police were called, and the doctors and nurses were looking everywhere for me. I knew they would call my mother and I felt sorry that I was giving her so much worry. I remember being very hungry as I was nil by mouth. I could see the hospital from where I had run to, and I saw a couple of police cars pull up. As young as I was, I knew they were there for me, and now I thought I was going to get into serious trouble.

Half an hour went by, and it seemed like a lifetime. That was when I knew I had no choice other than to return to the hospital. I headed in that direction, and in my white gown I stood out like a beacon, and I was spotted straight away by a policeman.

He was ever so good, and his kindness towards me made me feel better. He just put his arms out and said, 'Don't worry, boy. Everything is going to be okay.'

I thought at the time I was going to get shouted at, but everyone knew the situation I was in and I think they felt sorry for me.

When my mum turned up, she was just so glad to see me, that she never said a word about me running off. She guessed I had changed my mind. I think she was happy that I had, even though she didn't say so.

When we got home, Mum said, 'If it does get worse then we will need to go ahead with the operation, but for now we are going to leave it and just let nature take its course.'

CHAPTER THREE

Every other weekend, we would get into my mum's Mini, and drive down to London to see my mum's parents, Nan and Grandad Turvey. They lived opposite Euston train station, and it was an exciting place. My brother and I would play outside in the streets and sometimes wander over to the station, to watch the trains come and go.

My grandad had a lovely old dog that I used to play ball games with. He was a little Jack Russell. I loved that dog, and I knew that when I was older, I wanted to have my own dogs.

Our uncle Johnny, my mum's brother, would always be pissed in the local bar, so we didn't really see a lot of him when we went there.

On the way back home, we would go to Wembley Market. My mum searched out all the bargains, so we benefited from good fake clothes like La Shark, Fred Perry, Kappa and many other fake brands.

One place we always stopped at was the Indian Chicken Tikka van, as their food was very tasty. A family in our street who we were close to was an Indian family, who always brought homecooked food to us, as they knew my mum was a single parent. Their food was amazing, and they were such a lovely family and good friends of ours. They also had kids our age that we played with out in the street.

It was nice to have friends who were also neighbours, as my brother and I weren't close at all. It's a shame really, as I have always throughout my life wanted a brother or sister to be close to, so that we could love and look after each other and just be there. This wasn't the case with me and my brother, and as the years passed, we went our separate ways.

My mum always said I was like her, and my brother was more like our dad, but that never stopped her from loving us both the same. I know she took more time with me, but this was because of my disability and nothing else. We did share some friends together and we all went to the same places, but we didn't really mix easily with one another, even when we were out at the same places.

There have been moments in my life, when I have asked my brother to help me in the most horrible times. I'm not a person who likes asking for help, but I was at some of my lowest points where I really needed help, and I hoped that as his brother, I would be able to reach out to him.

One of these times was when I was homeless. I had made a huge mistake in my life, which I regret, and which had put me in the position of not having a roof over my head. In total despair I rang my brother for help, and I was hopeful that although we weren't close, he would help me because we were family.

I knew he was okay for money, as he ran his own business. I felt horrible having to ask for help, but he was my big brother, and the only one at that time that I felt I could turn to.

I explained my situation to him. It was really difficult and unpleasant, as I felt so low when I was telling him what had gone wrong, and how much I needed his help, but he never helped me at all.

When I got off the phone to him, I felt so upset, and I regretted opening up to him about all the trouble I was in because it was like he enjoyed it, or at least that's the impression I got.

The second time I asked him for help was when my life was threatened. I phoned a mutual friend, and after I told him about the trouble I was in, he said, 'Call your brother. I'm sure he will help you with this. I know he does nothing for you, but I am certain he will help this time.'

My brother and I hadn't spoken for ages, but I really needed help. It took me a lot to call him, but I braved it and made the call, and explained everything.

He knew I was in bits by the way I was talking, but as cold as he is, he turned me down, and said, 'Deal with it yourself.'

Hearing his words was like a knife going through my heart. The way he had rejected me without even a moment of consideration really did hurt me for a long time.

Now, I don't really even acknowledge that I have a brother, and that is a hard thing to admit to and to live with. He made his feelings clear about me, and I feel there is no going back from that. I don't want anything to do with him anymore. I know I will have a better life without him, which is sad but true.

I have never done anything towards him or hurt him in any way. All I ever wanted was to be close and love and help each other, like I see many other brothers and sisters doing, but it wasn't to be, and finally I accepted that.

CHAPTER FOUR

My schooldays were fun at first, until the real hard work started, and then I wasn't so keen. To begin with I went to this lovely little nursery. I remember when they used to shout, 'Drink time.' That was when we would all go and sit on a big square rug to eat our biscuits and drink our milk, out of the milk cartons they gave us. If one kid knocked his milk over, the whole class would shout out, 'Spilt milk', which everybody would find hilarious. Looking back now, I can only guess it was because of the age we all were at the time. It didn't take much to amuse us.

After Nursery, I moved up to the bigger part of the school, the primary school. I liked the school, but I wasn't very good at listening, and would easily lose myself in my own thoughts. If it was raining outside, I would totally drift off. I would watch it like I was transfixed, and I wouldn't even be aware of my surroundings. I could have been in the classroom or on the moon for all I knew.

I wasn't stupid but I wasn't brainy, I was just a normal, happy kid, but at school by the age of 9 years old, I was losing interest in studying and gaining interest in girls. Sitting behind a desk and being talked at by the teachers didn't appeal to me at all, as it was enough to send you to sleep.

It wouldn't have been so bad if they had allowed a bit of participation, but they just stood behind their desks, with us their captive audience, and it was awful. All I wanted was to be doing something active, and chasing the girls was definitely something I didn't get bored of! There was so much to learn about them, and I was leaning more and more all the time, and loving every minute of it.

I used to love 'kiss chase' in the playground, and I had one or two girlfriends, or at least as much of a girlfriend as you can have at that age. It's all very basic when you're that young. You ask her to be your girlfriend, she says yes, and that's it.

I often went on school trips, and one of them was to Cuffley Camp, where you would camp outside in these big forests. It was great, as I was used to my mum taking us camping. It was for three days and two nights, and it was the first time I had been away from Mum and I truly loved it, the great outdoors. We had big walks in the forest and singalongs at the campfires at night. I recall one school trip when my mum packed me a big bag of sweets. I felt devastated, when squirrels got into my tent and stole them.

But the older I got, the more disinterested I became in school and learning, as I had a very low boredom threshold.

I was glad when my mum met a new man, as I felt she deserved to have somebody to look after her. He was a good bloke and after a while he moved in with us. At first, he was a van delivery driver, then he and my mum set up their own window cleaning company which they ran in St Albans, where their customers were the ones who owned the very big houses.

I was 11 years old, and it was the beginning of the summer holidays. It was a time for a lot of changes, as after the holidays, I would be starting at big school, secondary school.

My new school was called the Lord Mountbatten School, which my brother attended already. It was named after Lord Louis Mountbatten, who was assassinated by the IRA in 1979, when they put a remotely controlled explosive device, underneath the ship he was on.

My mum's partner Ron became a part of all of our lives, and he was with us for quite a few years, so he was like our stepdad. He was very good to us and gave us all he could, and he treated us like we were his own children. He liked to travel which was good, as it gave me something in common with him, as I definitely had the travel bug.

He and my mum took us to places like Belgium, Holland, Germany, Italy, the Canary Islands, the Balearic Islands and mainland Spain. I have good memories of going to the lovely island Malta, and its smaller island Gozo next door. I was becoming well-travelled and I constantly marvelled at how the world was so big, with so many places to see and explore. I loved getting to know about all the different cultures and languages.

Even though my mum and Ron had their own business, their funds weren't limitless, so when a school skiing trip to Austria came up, I really wanted to go, but it was a bit too expensive. I told my mum that I would get a newspaper round, but I didn't stop there, as I was determined to go to Austria.

I asked the local milkman if he needed help in the mornings, and he agreed that I could work for him. I would be up at 5am and doing the milk round, before going to school. After school I would do my newspaper round, and I was saving every penny. For my age I was making good money, and I quickly realised that making money was much better than education and school.

I was really pleased when before my trip to Austria, a new dry ski run opened up next to my school. I put in plenty of practice on it to help me get ready for my trip to Austria. By the time the trip came around, I had saved up more than enough money and I was so excited.

We got there and it was amazing. The Alps were brilliant, and I was so pleased to ski on snow, which was much better than the dry ski slopes. I must admit though, that the only other thing I had on my mind apart from skiing, was girls.

One night the older sixth formers had gone out and bought some alcohol, and me and my friends managed to get some off them. It wasn't the first time I had tried alcohol, as close to our local shops there was a pub called The Cupid. I would go around the back with my friends, and we would crawl under the fence to get in. We would have a pole or stick with us, and then we would go and find the beer barrels. We used to push the pole or the stick down hard into the centre of the barrel, and all the beer would spray out, and we would get our mouths around it.

Back at the lodge we were staying in at the ski resort, things were heating up. We were knocking back the Vodka straight and playing kiss games with the girls like Spin the Bottle.

I thought it was amazing how the alcohol made me feel, but one of the other lads and a girl couldn't handle it. They were falling on the floor and the girl was being sick everywhere. It was a mess.

The hotel staff noticed it and reported it to the teachers, and we all had to go to bed early. We were given a right bollocking, but it didn't ruin my fun. From then on, I developed a liking for drink, and I wanted more.

Getting back to school after such an exciting holiday, made it seem even more boring than usual. I wasn't a really bad kid. I just used to mess about a lot, and it was putting other people off their work, so I was ending up in the headmaster's office quite often.

I was just a cheeky kid and didn't like to be told what to do, so I wasn't one of their favourite pupils. Despite not liking school, I fitted in well there. I wasn't a bully, but I knew how to handle myself. I did have quite a few fights throughout my school days, because I wasn't going to let anybody take liberties with me.

By this stage, I was desperate to leave school so that I could get out there and start earning some proper money. Finally, my messing about and not wanting to be told, ended with me back up in front of the headmaster yet again. It was the final straw, and I was expelled two weeks before the summer holidays.

My mum was a little upset with me, but I was her son, her angel, and she wanted me to be educated properly so that I could achieve great things when I left school. She spoke to the school board, and they said that after the school holidays they were going to try me at another school, where maybe I would fit in better. To me, it wasn't about fitting in. It was that I just didn't like school - full stop. But I was willing to give it another go for my mum's sake. I quickly put all that out of my mind, because I was still on school holidays, and it was party time.

CHAPTER FIVE

I was spending my time hanging around with a neighbour's son. His family owned a fruit and veg shop in Carpenter's Park. I was still doing my other little jobs, but his parents let me come and work in the shop with their son. I was loving life as now I had money coming in from everywhere.

When they were going on holiday to the South of France, they offered to take me with them. I asked my mum if I could go, and she said yes as she knew I loved camping and travelling, and she said I'd been good with all my jobs.

So, that was it, we were off and believe you me, we were OFFFFF! We were doing 140 mph in the RS Turbo more or less all the way down, and there were great tunes on too. I was buzzing. I believed that this was what life was all about, being in the fast lane.

We were heading for a campsite just outside St Tropez, and when we arrived life couldn't have been sweeter. We were doing BBQs every day, and his mum and dad turned a blind eye to us drinking the little bottles of Stella Artois, as long as we behaved ourselves and didn't go too crazy. I thought, come on we're teenagers! Going crazy is what we do!

His mum and dad were at the campsite swimming pool one day, when my friend decided to take their RS Turbo for a spin around the campsite. Of course, I was right there next to him!

We had the music turned up, and we were showing off with the windows all down when we went past these two hot French girls. We gave them a beep and a smile, and they smiled back and gave us a wave.

We decided to take the car back and go out and look for them. We grabbed a case of Stella. When we caught up with them, we discovered they didn't speak much English, and we didn't speak a word of French, but it was a great laugh. They weren't shy and before we knew it, they were half naked, and we were all over them.

After leaving the girls, we were full of drink and bravado. As far as I was concerned, life was good. Girls. Beer. Fast cars. What more could I ask for? Actually, on second thoughts, I could have asked for more, because I was still a virgin, but I was learning fast.

It was a fantastic holiday, and now we were heading back up through France with his parents, doing the normal fast speed, until my mate's dad blew the engine. The recovery truck came, and we ended up in a little place called Orange, and we had to stay in a hotel for two days, whilst waiting for parts for the car. When we finally arrived home, all I wanted was more.

But for now, the holidays were over and I was about to start my new school, Adeyfield. My head was still thinking about France, and I was thinking to myself that when I grew up, I was going to make it, and live abroad somewhere. That was going to be my future plan.

I tried my best to get on in my new school, but I just couldn't. My mind was on other things yet again. I was still getting told off and having to go and see the headmaster, but I felt I was trying my best.

All thoughts of making more effort at school flew out of the window, when I got friendly with the fittest girl in school.

I was 13 years old then, and she was two years older. I tried my best to see her and bump into her every day, and I could tell she had her eye on me too, as I was so cheeky and I had a great smile, if I do say so myself. Because I was tall, I looked older than my age, and I could get away with going into an off licence and buying a bottle of wine. It was much easier back in the days before all these photo IDs, and I would buy something like Thunderbirds. There were two kinds, a red label one and a blue one. The red one would get you shit-faced and the blue one just made you feel pretty good. I used to sometimes get bottles of 20/20 which did all the flavours.

One afternoon, I saw this older girl and asked what she was doing after school? And she said, 'Come round my house after. I'm not doing anything.' I thought, great, this is my chance to try and pull her. I knew where she lived as I had walked her home before, since it was the same route I took to go home.

After school, I went and got a bottle of blue label and knocked on her door. I had already done half a bottle and was in good spirits. She opened the door and I thought, you are fit as fuck. She said her parents were out and she asked, 'Would you like to come to my room to listen to some music?'

I was like, 'Let's go.' We had the music on, and she had a little of my drink. We were messing about and laughing, then we started to kiss. It was like heaven, and her body was fantastic. We got into bed and she showed me how to enter her and I was so hot. I had never felt like this before, it was magic. We went on having sex for a while, then all of a sudden, I went hotter, and felt like I was going to explode to be honest. I thought I was just about to piss myself inside her, and I pulled out, thinking, shit this is not going to be a good look. Seconds later, I realised I had cum. I was in heaven, like in a bubble, it was so nice. And she was too as she cleaned us both up. That's when I lost my virginity, and what a great person to lose it with. She was so hot and nice. Things did move quite quickly I know, but sometimes it does happen like that, and it's a nice thing and not bad in my eyes.

CHAPTER SIX

Hemel Hempstead was quite a nice place to live. At weekends I would meet with friends and go to the local cinema. I grew up on Star Wars movies, Rocky movies and many more. We had our own way of getting in. Two used to pay, then when inside, one would distract the person on the ticket booth, and one would open the fire exit door, so that we could all stream in without paying. Sometimes, we would get the train up to Milton Keynes to The Point entertainment complex because it had more choice, ten screens or twelve. They were good days out, with us all drinking and having a good time.

As for school, things weren't going well at all. I was hardly going, but I wasn't just bunking off and wasting time on the streets. I left my milk round job and got myself a job at the local market. I just loved the hustle and bustle, watching money getting exchanged everywhere and people buying off the stalls, together with the buzz of the market itself. It was definitely a bit of me.

I was still getting up at 5am and my first job there was on a pet stall, where I worked for an old man called Tom. My job was to set the stall up in the morning, and pack it all up again at the end of each day. If customers bought quite a few big items, I would help them get their new things back to the car. The fact that I would give them my cheeky talk and a big smile guaranteed that I would always get tips from them, in addition to my pay from Tom.

By the time I was 15 years old, school was behind me, and I was just making my own life and working hard at the market. With school over and done with, I was coining it in. This was my new life, and making money was what I enjoyed.

I started getting into fishing, and with all the money I was making, I was able to buy the equipment. Going fishing reminded me of when we were younger, and my mum and stepdad often took us to Stanborough Lakes at Welwyn Garden City. On one side you would watch people fishing, and on the other side you could feed the fish with pieces of bread. It was amazing, and I was hooked if you'll excuse the pun.

When I wasn't working, I would spend days and nights fishing at the lakes. The main fish I went for were carp. We used to pack our biffies, which are a kind of tent, all our equipment, loads of food, a mini cooker, beers and wines and more. We even had little parties when we fished. These were great days of my life.

There was one lake we fished at called Farlows Lake, which had a pub in the middle of the island. We'd have a pint or two there, and even a shower if we wanted to when we spent days there. Another lake I fished at was called Pixies Mere. It was a private lake which was membership only. I was a member, so I had a key to the gate, which allowed us to come and go as we pleased. I caught my biggest fish there, which was a twenty-four- pound common carp, and I was the happiest ever, and completely over the moon with my catch.

When I got into motorbikes, my mum wasn't keen. She didn't like them as she felt they were too dangerous, and she was right. Nevertheless, I bought one anyway, after spending a long time persuading my mum to agree to me getting one.

I already knew how to ride a motorbike as many of the other kids had them. My first bike was a Honda Super Dream 250cc. It was a heavy old bike, but I got it cheap. I know we were not all road legal, but we never took them out on the roads. We used to go to the woods right behind the house, or to a nearby farm, which was big with loads of private land.

Another thing we all got into was having air rifles. We would go over into the woods shooting them, and I became a very good shot. Sometimes, we would go for birds and other times we would take a load of tin cans to use.

We would practice in my mate's garden, but on one occasion, his neighbour said one pellet ricocheted and flew over their fence and nearly hit him, so he called the police. Immediately afterwards there were police everywhere and we were in big trouble. I know back then it probably wasn't viewed that way, but we were just normal kids experimenting and growing up. We were never setting out to hurt anybody.

I still had my market job during the day, but I started a cleaning job in the evening at Crompton Cleaning. It was two hours Monday to Friday, and they trained me up on the buffing machines. I enjoyed it and became quite good at it. I was glad for the extra money as I was saving up for my first tattoo, which I got a month later. I went to Dunstable to get it done and the man never asked for ID, which was good for me. Many of my friends also had tattoos. It was the in-thing to have, and I had no intention of lagging behind when it came to new trends.

I was beginning to hear a lot about a local nightclub called The Living Room, which was in the centre of Hemel Hempstead. It was a small nightclub which could hold a few hundred people. And boy, this nightclub did rock!

It was brilliant back in those days. Everybody knew everybody. It was like one big family in there. At first me and my mates just used to go drinking and dancing, but then we got introduced to Whizz (Speed) and LSD, and to some new and really good music. There was Rave music, House and Techno. It was different as it got you really hyped up and had really good bass lines and tweets. Growing up, I had been a big fan of the band Madness, so this music was a total change in direction, although I still enjoyed the earlier tunes I'd been fond of.

Later in life, I took my son to the Madness Concert at Fuengirola Bullring in Spain. We really did have a top night out and we took my Spanish teacher with us as she was a lovely lady, and I wanted to say thank you for all the Spanish lessons she gave me.

Once I was a regular at the Living Room, and had been introduced to drugs, I was just part of the crowd. Most people were taking them and were having the time of their lives, dancing to this hyped-up music. I knew drugs were dangerous and to keep clear of them, but I didn't think they could do much harm to me, even with my health problems.

We would start with Whizz and it was great. We would dance all night and we didn't get drunk anymore.

Even when we were still drinking it kept us awake. On the odd occasion we would take an LSD paper trip, which gave us lots of energy and made us laugh all the time, as we stood watching the lights and lasers in the club.

In those days, everyone was smoking weed, which I never really liked but plenty of my friends were smoking it. It just made me feel sick and go pale, so I left that alone. The Living Room nightclub was great back then, and we would go every week and dance the night away. In my case I couldn't stop dancing. That's why I got the name Lloyd of the Dance, or for short L.O.T.D.

We went to other nightclubs too in Watford, such as Paradise Lost, and a big pub called the Game Bird. We were young and just getting as much enjoyment as we could out of life. Back then there weren't strong weeds about like you get nowadays, and I hardly knew of anyone taking Cocaine. Now the place is awash with it.

Back in my day, there was Thai weed, and pot called soap and black, red and gold seal, but people were more interested in the Whizz and LSD, and the up-and-coming new pill called Ecstasy. This was the early 1990s and the rave club scene was kicking off big style.

CHAPTER SEVEN

Eventually, I decided to leave my job at the market, even though it was a job I enjoyed. Instead, I started working with my stepdad, window cleaning in St Albans, Radlett, London, Colney, and Hatfield. Business was improving for him, and he was getting busy, so I would help out one or two days in the week and on a Saturday. The good thing was, that I still had my cleaning job, which I did Monday to Friday evenings for two hours.

Things were beginning to look up. Now I was old enough to get my motorbike licence and go on the roads. I sold my old Super Dream 250cc and I bought a red and white DT 50cc. It cost more than I could afford, so my mum paid the rest and paid for my insurance. I passed my test with flying colours and I was buzzing, I was so happy. Now I could go anywhere, and I felt so free it was amazing.

I had just made a friend at my cleaning job, and after work we would go and play snooker. There was a big snooker hall on the local parade of shops, and it had fifteen full sized tables, so it was great going for a game and a pint. Next door was the Cupid bar, which is the same place where me and my mates as kids would puncture the barrels and swig the beer that came pouring out.

Now I was growing up, it became one of my locals. In the middle of the two locals was a bookmaker, and eventually I started going in there to have a flutter. I wasn't a big gambler, but I loved the buzz of winning. My main game was the dogs and then the horses. As I carried on with my gambling, I became a known face at Wembley Dog Track, which in those days was based at Wembley Football Stadium. Sadly, the dog track has been closed down now for years and is finished.

My other favourite was Walthamstow Dog Stadium, as it was a top night out. If I won, I would go to a nightclub called Charlie Chan's, which was underneath the track, and I got to know loads of people there. I also followed horse racing at Kempton Park, Ascot and many more, but these two were the main ones, and Ladies Day was always a favourite.

I know they say that all gamblers are losers, but I had my moments, and one of them was when I went for a weekend away to Bournemouth with a couple of friends. On our last day, we were all skint, but I put a bet on at the bookies. I put a pound on a place pot and chose six horses, and guess what, all six horses came in, bringing me a total win of £1,630. Once that money was in my hands that was good reason to stay a bit longer, and I paid the hotel for two more nights. We hit the bars and a nightclub called The Cage. We really did have a top time. But even though I was enjoying myself, I knew better than to blow the lot. I had always been a saver, so I did keep some money back for when I went home.

At the snooker hall I met another friend, who was a few years older than me. This wasn't unusual as most of my friends were older than me. He had a big American van, a bit like the A Team van with sliding doors, and he was a massive pot head. We would go on drives around the local area, and during our travels we met two girls. I became very fond of one of them and we started to date, and that was the start of things to come.

We had been seeing each other a long time when she became pregnant. We were both happy and in love, but both young, and it was a bit of a shock to realise that we were about to start a family. I left my mum's house and rented a room at my mate's house, so that I could start living a responsible life.

I had the full backing of my mum, who was glad that I was taking my responsibilities seriously. I was still doing my jobs and had my DT 50cc motorbike for transport, so life was good.

When my girlfriend and I split up briefly, I went off the rails a bit, and put all my concentration into enjoying myself. I was still going to The Living Room nightclub, where I would dance and take drugs. On one occasion, me and my friends started at their flat before we went to the nightclub. We all took a paper LSD trip which went very wrong.

I thought I was some sort of superman and started going crazy. I went to the flat window and tried to jump out of the upper floor that we were on. I am so lucky that my friends grabbed me back and saved me. Then, I started to fight them and got out of the flat door and ran off down the street, where I took my clothes off before jumping into a water fountain. The police had already been alerted and were on their way, and my mum was called by a friend.

It was a bad trip, and I am lucky to be alive, thanks to my friends and the police. I woke up in a hospital bed with drips coming out of me. The trip was so strong that I overdosed on it. My mum came to see me, and I was still shaking. It was so scary that I wouldn't wish it on anyone. I was so upset about what I had put my mum and my pregnant girlfriend through, not to mention the police and the hospital. I was really embarrassed and so sorry for what I had done. I wouldn't have done it if I had known this would happen, but that's the thing with drugs, you can never tell, which is why they are so dangerous. From that day on I never went near LSD again.

After what happened, my mum wanted to keep a close eye on me. She was leaving on a holiday trip to the South of France and Italy, with my stepdad, in the new car they had just got. Mum begged me to go with them, as she didn't want to leave me behind after what had happened. I wasn't supposed to go with them, but my mum was so worried about me, that she was determined to do her best to organise it so that I could as well, even though it was short notice.

I didn't need too much persuading, so I decided to go with them, as I wanted to get my life back on track. After the ordeal I'd been through, I thought that good food and sun would help me, and it turned out be just what I needed.

We arrived in Milan in Italy, and we went to see all the sights and visited Tuscany. We saw the Leaning Tower of Pisa, and then headed up to the South of France, where we stayed in Monaco, which is famous for its Grand Prix where they race through the streets. We drove around the streets where the Grand Prix takes place and went through the same tunnel that they drive through. I just loved the place. I was impressed by the wealth and all the boats in the Marina, and I was sure that one day I would be able to afford those things.

Later in life, I became friends with a man who I met at the Byblos Hotel. It is very well known in Spain. It's on the Mijas Golf Course and I used to play golf there. It's a place where it's said the King of Spain and also the late Princess Diana stayed. It's an elite Hotel with helicopter access.

I met the man in the hotel bar and found out that he was very wealthy, with property in Spain and also in Guernsey and Jersey. We became good friends and always met up for gin and tonics at the bar. Sometimes we would go out for a meal and he would never let me put my hand in my pocket. He was a very generous man.

He told me about his boat in Monaco harbour which overlooks the streets where the Grand Prix takes place, and he invited me to go to Monaco with him and his wife and some of their friends. We were to fly there in his own private Learjet. It all sounded amazing, and it was something I would have liked to have done, but I already had a big trip booked to Asia, so unfortunately, I had to decline his offer. I am still friends with him now but don't see him very often. Sadly, his wife died and afterwards he became an alcoholic. I was glad to hear at a later date though, that he conquered his alcoholism.

When I arrived back from my holiday with my mum, I was fresh, strong and healthy, and now I was back with my girlfriend. She told me that she was due to have a little baby girl, and we were both over the moon. I took her to a Beefeater restaurant to celebrate, as we loved going for meals there.

I was approaching the age when I would be eligible to get a driving licence, and I was anxious to get it. I knew it would be a great help to have a car with a family on the way, but I'd not even had any driving lessons yet. My mum got me insured on her car and used to take me to the industrial estate, so she could teach me to drive in a safe environment. She was so calm with me that I thought she should have been a driving instructor! I learnt very easily with her.

When I'd had a few lessons, and had got the hang of it, we decided that we would call a driving school, so that I could start lessons with them. To my amazement, the driving instructor told me after two lessons, that I didn't need any more. He said that he would put me forward for a driving test. He praised my mum's teaching, as he thought she had done amazingly well to get me to the standard I was at. Mum was very pleased when I told her what he'd said.

Shortly afterwards I took my test in St Albans. I was nervous but I managed to stay composed, and it went well. When I was told that I had passed, I felt as though I'd suddenly been given the freedom, to go wherever I wanted with family and friends.

CHAPTER EIGHT

The rave and club scene had become massive at this point, and despite my overdose, I didn't want to give up on going dancing and listening to the music. I often travelled to London and went to great venues, like The Orange at the Rocket on Holloway Road, just past the Kiss FM Studio. It was brilliant and we would have a top night in there dancing until six in the morning. Also, there was Camden Palace, which was a top nightspot.

The Gas Club was another one I went to, and Manny, a good mate of mine worked on the door. He was from Hemel Hempstead too and was a very hard man. He's in his fifties now and still does unlicenced boxing. The Ministry of Sound at Elephant and Castle was also good. Later in life, I went to the Ministry of Sound in Bulgaria in Sunny Beach. That was definitely worth a few visits, as the atmosphere was amazing and so were the girls. The Ministry of Sound in Spain was at Fuengirola Castle down by the beach, and it was another good place to go.

The one club which gets a special mention was the club of all clubs, which was called Labyrinth and was at 12 Dalston Lane in Hackney. I knew Joe who owned the place, and it really was something else. It was underground in what seemed like dungeons, and the music system was powerful. The entire place used to shake with the vibrations from it. This place was for die-hard ravers.

The sweat from the heat of people's bodies dripped off the ceilings, and everybody was dancing endlessly. If it became too hot, there was a little garden, you could pop out to and cool off, and you could even have a spliff out there if you wanted to. The place was wicked and everybody who went there thought so too. The DJs were some of the best around. There were people like Billy Bunter, Vinyl Matt,

Groove Rider and Rat Pack. The music really was first class. I bumped into Roland in this club, and Ginge, the ones who starred in the Grange Hill television series back in those days. This club was truly the best, and I had some of my best ever nights in there.

I was growing up fast, maybe too fast some might say, but sometimes that's how it goes. I stopped my cleaning job at Crompton Cleaning, and I started with a recruitment agency who got me a full-time job with B.O.C, which was night work, starting at 7pm and finishing at 5am. I really liked the job and met some great and funny people. The job I did was working in a massive freezer, where I picked and packed frozen food for Marks and Spencers.

While working there, I got to know a colleague, who also liked Whizz. He did the same job as me, and we had to pick and pack, then load the pallets up and get them ready to be put on the lorries, to go to the stores. It was hard work, and there were about one hundred of us doing the late shift.

Before long, everybody who worked alongside us started taking Whizz. Our boss couldn't work out why suddenly we were working so quickly. Our team was finishing about 4am or even 3am sometimes, but we still got paid up to 5am. It was so funny the way we were all running around like Billy Whizz, shooting here, running there and doing everything so fast. When we finished work, we played cards and waited for the other teams to finish, and we were taking home good money.

During this time, I managed to save up to buy my first caravan. My daughter was born, and we were all very excited. When I laid eyes on her, I thought she was so beautiful, and I was proud to have such a lovely daughter in my life.

We took the caravan up to Billing Aquadrome in Northampton, which is a massive holiday park with bars, restaurant, funfairs, fishing lakes and sports lakes for jet-skiing and much more. We fell in love with the place, and decided to pitch our caravan up there permanently, so that we could travel there at weekends. I even ended up getting a Mitsubishi short wheelbase jeep, which was better for towing, and nice and spacious for the family.

Just over a year later, my girlfriend was pregnant with our second child and we were so excited, especially when we found out we were having a boy. I was looking forward to having a real little mini me. When my son was born, we celebrated, and I could see straight away that he had a very strong resemblance to me.

After a while, we sold the caravan and bought a static mobile home in Northampton, where we spent lots more times, and made some wonderful memories. We also went on holidays to Tenerife and Menorca so the kids could start enjoying travelling as much as I did.

Back in Hemel Hempstead, I left my job at B.O.C, and I started to buy and sell second-hand cars. I and would go to the auctions and study the Auto Trader magazine. I also set up a little valeting service called Wright Shine, as I was fed up with working for other people. I decided it was time to go it alone, but I knew you had to have balls to do this, and I had them alright.

CHAPTER NINE

Sadly, after a few years, my girlfriend and I split up. We had tried so many times to work things out between us, but it wasn't to be. Maybe we did start too early, but what we had out of it was two lovely kids and we both stayed close friends. I will always love her as she is the mother of my kids and we have remained very close, even today. I was so happy that I had my kids with her, she truly is a top woman and I admire her. She has now gone on to have two more kids with her new man, so now my daughter and son have two half-sisters.

After splitting up with my girlfriend, I carried on doing my work and tried to keep myself busy. I used to have the kids every other weekend and every Wednesday night. I would take them out for their favourite pizza, and we would go to places like Zizzi pizza restaurant at St Albans, which was one of our favourites. Their food is truly delicious. Our other favourite was Pizza Express in Harpenden.

I bought my son a mini quadbike and took him to the fields to ride it, and I also watched him play football at weekends. When my mate told me that he was taking his daughter to Disneyland in Florida, I said I would love to take my daughter as she wanted to go there. In the end, we all went for ten days and it was amazing, watching the girls having so much fun. Even me and my mate did. It really is a magical place.

I had grown out of going raving, but on the odd occasion I would have a blowout and go dancing, but at the opposite end of the scale I was particularly interested in golf. I sold my static mobile home in Northampton, and with help from my mum and stepdad, I bought a lovely static residential mobile home in Bedmond, Abbots Langley, close to Kings Langley and Watford, just off the M25. It was a beautiful home with a lovely little garden, which I always took pride in.

Just around the corner from there, was Shendish Manor House which had an 18 Hole golf course. I started to play there with some friends. One of them is called Norm, and he is like a true brother to me and always has been. We played some really good rounds of golf there. Another one of our favourite places was Lammarwood up past Harpenden. It was owned by a Japanese family, and we always used to visit their restaurant after a round of golf.

The good thing about buying and living in a static mobile home is the bills. You own your mobile home, so you have no mortgage, and all you have to pay are your bills and ground rent for the site. Back then it was only £78 a month and my heating and water bills were extremely small.

Around this time, I made another friend, who became a very close buddy of mine. He sold cars on a very grand scale. I had recently started going to Chelsea football games, and I was meeting more new friends from all around the country. Most of them were criminals although some were just law-abiding businessmen. It didn't matter to me either way, as it was the friendship that mattered, not what they did for a living.

There was a trip coming up to go to Sweden to watch football. It was the Cup Winners Cup, Chelsea versus Stuttgart, a German team, and it was being played in Stockholm. A few of us wanted to go and make a holiday out of it, and while in Sweden play some golf too. We decided to rent a mobile home, and drive to Sweden. It was going to be a very memorable trip which we would all enjoy.

We stopped in Amsterdam, did the red-light district, watched some live sex shows and got drunk in the Bulldog bars. We ate some space cakes, which is when pot is put into cakes, so we were stoned and laughing, and having a good time.

Our next stop was Hamburg in Germany, and ended up in a strip club where things turned nasty. One of my mates named Matt ordered a small bottle of sparkling wine, which was a bit like cheap champagne, and one of the girls said he had to pay £300 for it. We were outraged and we were having none of it. The doorman was called but we still refused to pay. It was all about to kick off big time, but one of the doormen just told us to leave, so we left without paying anything. They were well aware that we were up for a ruck, and it must have been very clear to them that we weren't about to be mugged off. So that was the end of that. My mates are big Chelsea boys and they don't take any shit!

Next stop was Denmark, where we found a nice little campsite that had a bar and a BBQ. After that we ended up in Stockholm and we painted the city Blue. 'Come on Chelsea,' we roared, as we walked through the city. The game started and we won 2-1 and there was a great goal by the legend Zola. We got to play some golf too while we were in Sweden. But this wasn't going to be my last time there.

Years later I did a removal to Sweden from Malaga, Spain. It was for a friend of mine who owned Tramps Bar in Fuengirola. He wanted to move back to Sweden as he had been born there. What a mare me and my mate had! We had never done this sort of work before, and from start to finish it went wrong, and we under-priced the whole job.

We rented a big van from Convoy Rentals in Malaga. We packed the van up with all the belongings, and that was a job in itself. We hadn't realised how hard it would be up and down stairs with furniture in boiling hot weather. We both felt absolutely fucked by the time we'd finished loading.

We headed off up the coastline, and along the way everything went very dark. A massive storm was brewing and when it rains in Spain it rains. The rain started coming down very heavily and turned into flash floods.

Fortunately, there wasn't much traffic on the roads. As we approached Murcia, I noticed the brakes had gone. I had the pedal right down and nothing was happening. We were doing about 60mph and this was too fast to pull the handbrake up to bring us to a standstill. We had no alternative, other than to wait until we came to a natural stop.

If there had been a traffic jam, or any other reason for the traffic to suddenly come to a halt, we would have just smashed into whatever was in front of us, causing fatalities which would have included ourselves. We were shitting ourselves, and we didn't have a clue what to do! We were glad when eventually we ran out of speed. That was when we managed to manoeuvre ourselves into a petrol station.

We rang the rental company and explained angrily what had happened. They sent us a pick-up recovery truck. Our van was an Iveco van, and strangely the place where we had managed to come to a standstill, had a main outlet Iveco garage on the other side of the road! The rental company paid for a taxi to take us to a hotel, which they also paid for. When I got there, I immediately recognised it. I had this feeling of déjà vu. Everything seemed familiar, but I wasn't quite sure why. When eventually I realised the reason for this, I couldn't quite believe it. Ten years earlier when I was heading to Spain, I broke down in the very same area, and it was the same hotel, that I had ended up at!

The next day the garage finished repairing the van and we got it back. Soon afterwards we were on our way. We got to Alicante way and went through the toll there and paid. We were just pulling away from there when we noticed two police motorbikes and a police car following us. I knew what was going to happen and I wasn't wrong. The sirens and the lights went on, so I pulled over. They could see it was a rental van, as this was written on the side. When they found out we were English, they wanted to search and weigh it.

I knew that the police were thinking. Because we were English and in a rental van heading to Sweden, we must be drug smugglers, as this was a major route for the drug smuggling trade. They took us to a weighbridge, and we were gutted to find we were overweight. They fined us 800

Euros, which pissed us off, and they made us take everything off the van to be searched, before allowing us to put it back on. As we were driving away, we felt our journey was just doomed. Everything was going wrong; brakes, police, fines. What next?

When we got to Denmark, we must have hit the worst weather ever! The gusts of wind were so bad, that the van would have toppled over for sure if we had gone any faster than 40 mph. It took us ages to get through Denmark and we still had to get to the top of Sweden. It was bad and dangerous weather all the way up, and just added to our misery.

Finally, we made our drop, got paid, and headed back down to Malaga. That was when we realised that the entire job had cost us more than we earned. We had been gone nine days and only spent two of them in a hotel. The rest of the time we slept in the van to save money. It hadn't been one of our better ideas, and we certainly learned an expensive and uncomfortable lesson!

CHAPTER TEN

Once I was back in Bedmond living in my mobile home, I was enjoying it so much that I felt like I was on holiday. I had met an air stewardess who worked for KLM Airlines, and she was very beautiful. She lived in Wilmslow, Cheshire, which is not far from Manchester. Spending a bit of time in a new area appealed to me, so I went up there and spent time with her. It was enjoyable but things never worked out between us, so it wasn't long before I was back to being single.

Not long afterwards, I was out drinking at a bar called The Leather Bottle, when I bumped into a girl that I already knew. We hit it off straight away. She was single too, and she ended up back at my mobile home, and you know the saying *don't come knocking when the caravan is rocking*. We had a very passionate night, and soon fell for each other. This was the start of a serious relationship, and within two weeks she had practically moved in with me. We were in love and spent all our time together.

She had a good job at Bentley Cars in Bovingdon. I met her parents and they treated me like family, and we all went on holidays together. I played golf in Portugal with her dad, and I also took him to the World Cup football in France, and the Euros in Holland. I was always around their house for dinners, and I was included in all the special occasions. My girlfriend got us tickets to see Lord of the Dance, which was great, and she also took me to places that she found through Red Letter Events, which do good discounts on different activities. One of the events involved me racing around Brands Hatch all weekend which was fantastic, and I appreciated her thoughtfulness.

Like me, she was born with a disability, as her hips and pelvis had broken at birth. When I met her, she was on her second hip replacement and was awaiting her third. As she was so young, she was having hip replacements which only lasted 7-10 years. I used to take her to the hospital specialist down in London at Stanmore Orthopaedic Hospital. She was so understanding with my disability that we were like a perfect match.

She was great with my kids and my mum, and we took them on holidays too. I was a regular at a pub nearby, called The Swan. We would go there every day to have drinks with friends or a meal. I felt as though my life was complete, and it seemed as though nothing could go wrong.

Then some news came to my attention, which made me feel very uncomfortable. Rumour had it that a couple of weeks before my girlfriend started seeing me, she had met my brother at a party, and had slept with him. Despite knowing that if it did happen, it was before she and I got together, the thought of it didn't sit right with me. I decided to ask my brother about it, and first of all he said he had, then he changed his mind and said he hadn't. All I wanted was the truth.

I asked her and she said no she hadn't slept with him, so we carried on with our lives. But there was always something in the back of my mind about that situation. It began to eat me up, but I still tried to ignore it, and carry on enjoying my life with her.

She had her new hip replacement and stayed in hospital for nearly two weeks. Afterwards, she took a year out of work to recover and I was there with her every day, to give her all the support and love she needed.

I prepared the mobile home for when she came back. She had a wheelchair for going out and about, and crutches when we were indoors. For the first six weeks after she came back, we just stayed at home relaxing. I would spend lots of time caring for her and doing the garden outside, and she would just sit and watch me. After that we started to go out and I saw an advertisement in the newspaper, about a hotel down in Folkestone called The Grand Burstin Hotel, which was good for older people and had wheelchair facilities.

It was close to Dover, and to Calais, so we could pop over there and get booze and shopping. Every two weeks we went there to stay. There was plenty of entertainment at the hotel, and there was a great view of the harbour and the old Russian submarine which was ported there as a museum. I loved the big bags of whelks and prawns from the local seafood vans, and even though my girlfriend was recovering from a major operation, we still had a good time.

I was still selling second-hand cars and operating my valeting service. I also managed to do a little business with a friend who was selling glass conservatories. I agreed to put customers his way, in return for some cash. I made a few deals and sold four of his conservatories to friends, so I was owed quite a few quid. I still hadn't received the money, but my friend was selling his motorhome, and he liked one of the cars I was selling, so we made a deal. I wouldn't be paid in cash for the custom I'd got him. Instead, I had the motorhome off him, and he had one of my cars.

So, me and my girlfriend planned a trip to the South of France in our motorhome, and spent a month there living on campsites. We ended up spending more time in France than in England, and I thought that I wouldn't mind living there at some point in the future.

CHAPTER ELEVEN

I had started doing money lending with 10% interest on top, so every £1,000 I loaned, I would get back £1,100. The arrangement was that I would only loan it for a month.

One bloke I knew was a highflyer who worked at the Stock Exchange and lived in a private gated address, in the very posh end of Harpenden. He was a wealthy man who loved Cocaine, girls and partying. He'd borrowed money off me before, so I wasn't surprised to hear from him.

It was early morning when I woke up and noticed I had missed calls from him. I rang him back and asked him if he was okay, and how much he needed. I couldn't get much sense out of him as he was drunk and high on Cocaine. I thought he was asking me for ten grand, and I asked him if he was sure this was the amount he wanted. He said it was. I had just sold a car for a good price, so I had enough to lend him the money.

Usually, I wouldn't have large sums of money like that just lying around. It was the most he had ever asked for, but I counted it out in fifty-pound notes so it wasn't a massive bundle, and I put it in a bag and tied it before taking it to him. I knocked on the door and a beautiful half naked girl answered the door. He didn't come to the door, but he shouted out for me to just give her the money, which I did. I didn't hear from him for the next few days, but after a big party I knew he always liked to recover at home.

A few days later, I was sitting in my local, The Swan, and he came in by himself. I went over and asked how he was, and when he would be repaying me. As we were chatting, I said, 'Mate, what the fuck were you doing? That was a lot of money for a night with a hooker.'

He laughed, and said, 'It was only two grand, and that's nothing.'

I replied, 'What the fuck are you talking about? You said ten grand, not two. I asked you again on the phone if you were sure you wanted that much, and you said yes, so I put the ten grand in fifties into the bag and paid the girl.'

He went the palest I've ever seen someone go. It turned out that he was so pissed and high when he spoke to me on the phone, that he didn't realise he'd said ten grand. He immediately contacted the escort agency, who knew him to be a good customer. He told them what had happened, and they explained that the girl he'd been with was a new girl who had only just started working for them. They said she had been off work for a few days after the party with him.

They rang her and she admitted that she had counted the money and obviously knew there was ten grand there. She said she was scared that they were checking her out and it had all been a set up with the money.

Bullshit, I thought. Give it a couple of weeks and if nobody had asked for it back, she would have spent it. I must admit I was surprised she just hadn't done a runner with it. Fortunately, she still had the money, and after taking her two grand out, she gave the rest back to my mate, and he paid it all back to me.

Me and my girlfriend had not long returned from holiday, so that she could have her hospital check-ups, but immediately afterwards, we headed off to the Dominican Republic, where there are the most beautiful, white sandy beaches. We booked an all-inclusive resort with good wheelchair access. It was close to the beach and had many restaurants and good nightlife.

We had been with each other for quite a while now, even though that thing with my brother was still playing on my mind, but she continued to deny that it had happened.

While we were in the Caribbean, I bought her a beautiful white gold and diamond engagement ring, and I proposed by the swimming pool. She said yes, and we celebrated with a meal, a bottle of wine, and lots of passion later that night.

Once we went back home, I continued selling cars, and I spent a lot of time at my local, The Swan. There, I met another one of my good friends, Mark Walsh. He was a talented darts player and was one of the top five UK players. We practiced together and unsurprisingly, he always won. I went to watch him play a few times when he was on the television, at the Circus Tavern near Lakeside Shopping Centre.

I had been with my girlfriend for nearly two years, and she had recovered fully from her operation. We had a meeting with the local vicar, as we had chosen the beautiful local church nearby in Abbot's Langley for our wedding. We preferred to have it in the summer because of the bad British weather. The wedding ceremony was arranged for five months later. It was now February, so we had loads of time for planning our fabulous day.

I happened to meet a friend of mine who I hadn't seen for a while. He was also a friend of my brother. The subject came up about what had happened that night with my girlfriend and my brother, and he said, '100% it did happen.'

He saw the shock on my face, and he said he always thought I knew about it. My head went into overdrive and I felt really sad. A couple of weeks passed and during that time I was distant with my girlfriend.

I took her out for a meal, and I said, 'Look, we're getting married, so let's not hold anything back. Let's have the truth on the subject of my brother before we tie the knot.'

In my heart, despite what my friend had said, I still believed she hadn't slept with my brother, because of all the times she had denied it. I was worried when she went quiet and started to cry. I thought she was just going to admit to a little bit more than a kiss with him.

I was stunned when she said, 'Yes, we did go all the way.'

I felt as though my heart had stopped, and my world was falling apart. I didn't really say much in response, but after we got home, I was really quiet and offish for about a week.

I knew I just couldn't carry on with her, despite my best efforts. I tried to convince myself that I would get over it in time, and everything would be alright, but it was no good. I couldn't get it off my mind. What made it worse was all the times she had denied it. I ended things with her, and it broke both our hearts.

CHAPTER TWELVE

It took a long time, but I moved on in life and also moved out of my mobile home into a cottage. I completed the paperwork at the post office, so that I could change the name to *Wrighty's Cottage*. It was still in the same area and I was getting on with life as best I could.

There was another big wedding coming up of a good friend of mine who was a Chelsea fan like me. He was due to get married and he invited me on his stag weekend. We went on a long stay weekend to New York. He was a well-known man and a big face around Chelsea, and he paid for the flights and hotel.

This was just what I needed to take my mind off things. We landed at JFK, and had the limos pick us up. We had to wait for another flight to land, as all our Dutch Chelsea supporters were part of the stag party too. The limos took us to our hotel in the centre of New York. There must have been about fourteen of us in two limos.

But what we didn't know was on that particular weekend, there was a massive gay event being held in the area. There we were, fourteen big Chelsea blokes, all drinking champagne in the limos, and as we turned a corner, we had to stop to let the marchers through. Suddenly, we were spotted in the limos by a group of about twenty gay men, who obviously thought we were gay too. They came up to the windows and welcomed us to New York, with plenty of flirtation in their voices.

We had definitely picked the wrong weekend! Instead of girls all over the place, there were men everywhere you looked!

Two of the brothers who were on the stag weekend had contacts in New York, and they and others wanted some weed and other party things. They called their contacts, and within an hour the stuff had been dropped off.

We all headed off for a trip down to the Marina, to get a boat to go and see the Statue of Liberty. There were loads of tourists, but mainly men, and most of the boats were slow and too boring for a stag party. Then we came across a big bright yellow speed boat, which was advertising itself as the fastest speedboat in New York. The owner was a huge American bloke who was an ex- WWF wrestler, who had retired because of health problems, and had bought the boat. We went out on his speed boat and around the Statue of Liberty a few times. We took lots of photos, and then he said, 'You wanna see this baddy open up?'

Of course, we wanted him to go as fast as he could, and by the size of the engines of this speed boat, this thing could rip. He told us that he still had to be careful as many police speed boats were about, and they would fine him if they saw he was over the speed limit.

We just encouraged him to do it anyway, and before we knew it, we were speeding around and having the time of our lives. Suddenly, we were spotted by a police speed boat, which was now coming for us with lights on and siren going. We were worried as it started to chase us, and we didn't realise this was part of the show, that the owner of the speedboat always put on, to give the tourists a thrill-seeking adventure. Everybody started throwing their weed and other drugs overboard, and it wasn't until we got back to the Marina, that we realised it was all part of the show! When the police speed boat came alongside us and the police laughed, it really was tops and the boys saw the funny side. One of our group was a little pissed off, as he had thrown his stash overboard thinking it was real police chase, and didn't want to be nicked, especially in New York.

We had a great time, and we also saw the Twin Towers before the world went crazy and the planes deliberately crashed into them. We also saw the Empire State Building and went up in it.

After the stag weekend, I was finding it lonely at home without a girlfriend, so I decided to get a dog. I'd always wanted one, so I bought myself a British Bulldog and named him Boss. He meant the world to me and the kids loved him too. I had a lovely little back garden for him, and there were beautiful walks over the woods that we used to go on, and he would come to the local pubs with me. Everyone loved him and he was a true companion and so affectionate.

A friend of mine and his dog used to meet up in different areas for walks. His dog was called Hugo. This particular day, we decided to meet up at Ashridge Forest, which was a lovely place to walk, and deer could be seen there.

When we got there, we were enjoying the peace of the walk, until Hugo saw a small deer, and ran after it with Boss following him. We started to shout them back, 'Hugo, Boss, Hugo, Boss!' Then we noticed this lady with her poodle dog. Our dogs had come back by then, so we thought we would go over and greet the lady and her dog. When we got close, she was shouting her dog's name, or so we thought.

'Gucci, Gucci,' she yelled. We thought it was brilliant that she had named her dog after a designer label, so when we got close, we said, 'Nice name for your dog.'

It turned out that Gucci wasn't the name of her dog. She had heard us shouting Hugo and Boss, so she decided to make fun of us by pretending her dog was also named after a designer. We all found it very funny, and the three of us walked our dogs together that day.

I was single for quite a while, and not really looking for anyone, and I had plenty of time on my hands. When I heard that the dad of a friend of mine had died, I was sad as I was a good friend of the dad as well as the son.

I'd taken the dad on fishing trips, and we used to pick up cars together that I cleaned or sold. He truly was a dear old man. He owned a massive yard where I used to park my motorhome, and park cars there when I ran out of space in front of the cottage. I had also taken him to mainland Spain once with his sons.

The wake was at my local, The Swan. It really was a great turnout; so many people and a great send off. This is where I met another love of my life and she too was an air stewardess, who lived in Essex, quite close to Stansted Airport. I must have been a sucker for air stewardesses! I'd had one before from Manchester, and another one I met in Cyprus at Ayia Napa. She was from New Zealand and wanted me to go over there, but at the time I felt it was too far.

Me and this new girl hit it off straight away and were soon dating. She would come and stay at the cottage, or I would go to Essex, but her parents didn't like me.

We used to go into London a lot, or to the countryside for weekends away. About this time too, my family had bought a lovely little one-bedroom apartment in mainland Spain on Mijas Golf, so we used to stay there too. We really were enjoying ourselves and falling for each other, and we spent lots of time at my local, The Swan pub, where we first met.

I was doing a lot of work with cars, together with my multi-millionaire friend. He had loads of cars and I used to buy and sell them from him, but as well as that, he was one of my closest friends. We used to go on skiing holidays together to Switzerland and Italy, and he was a good bloke.

My girlfriend and I had booked a trip to Tunisia, and actually we stayed quite close to the area where those terrorists shot people down on the beach. My girlfriend didn't like it much there, as being a beautiful blonde, all the men would stare at her. One day she stayed around the pool and I went out on the piss. As I was leaving the complex, I asked the gateman where I could find a good bar.

'Turn left,' he said. 'There are some good bars that way, but don't go right, and to the bar down there. It's a bad bar.' I thought, sod that, I want adventure. I wanna see the bad bar. So off I went.

When I entered the bar, I noticed quite a few blokes about. There was music on, and a pool table. I got into the spirit and necked a few drinks and shots as I was in the holiday mood. There were a few of them playing pool, so I said, 'I will play the winner.'

I was soon beating them all, and the whole bar was watching me playing. They were clapping and patting me on my shoulder, and really watching me bend over the table for all my shots, and everyone was quite excited with the games going on.

There's nothing wrong with this bar, I thought. They are all very happy people. They were a bit touchy and over friendly, but I thought nothing of it.

Later that night when I was drinking back at the hotel bar, I explained to the local barman where I had been. He said, 'Oh no, you were in a gay bar!' That's when I realised why they had been so touchy feely in the bar.

Back in the UK things were good between me and my girlfriend, though her parents were telling her to keep away from me, as they just didn't like me from the start. Their attitude began to affect our relationship, and in addition to that, I was unaware that one of my best mates was texting her. It was my multi-millionaire friend texting her and he kept telling her that they would look good together in his jacuzzi.

Unaware that this was going on, I thought I would arrange a surprise for her parents to win them over. I went to a travel agent and booked a mind-blowing holiday. It started in San Francisco then onto Las Vegas, and then Los Angeles. It was to be First Class all the way with great hotels. I got the tickets and some flowers and went to Essex to tell them what I'd organised.

I thought it went well, but I still didn't feel I had won them over. A couple of weeks passed, and the holiday was coming up, and still, I knew nothing about these text messages.

Then a week or so before we were due to start our holiday, she said, 'Sorry, I can't go with you.'

I was in shock and I was broken hearted, when she finally told me about the texts. I couldn't quite believe it at first. 'He's one of my best mates.'

Then she showed me some of them, and said, 'I am sorry, but I'm confused. I don't want to be with either of you for now. I want to be on my own.'

I said, 'You're mad if you go with him, because I am sure it will only be for money, and not for love.'

She replied, 'I just want to be alone.'

I'm sure they're still trying to put her off me and that, together with my best mate's antics, were enough to make her unsure. I never said anything to him as I thought it would blow things up unnecessarily. I believed that she would change her mind and be back with me. Nothing happened. I called her at the end of the week but still she hadn't changed her mind.

I still had this holiday coming up. I had spent a lot of money which would just be wasted now. I asked for a refund but because it was so close to the date of departure, they refused. I could have a little back, but it wasn't worth it. I rang loads of people and asked who wanted a free holiday. There was only four days to go. I thought it would be easy to find someone for a free first-class holiday to the USA, but because it was at short notice, most people were already committed to work and other things.

Eventually, I found a friend of mine who wanted to go with me. So, the holiday was on and I needed it, as all the shit going on with me splitting up, and this prick of a supposed best friend of mine, trying to snatch my girlfriend, had made me feel very down. I wasn't going to let them break me down and spoil my holiday.

CHAPTER THIRTEEN

And what a holiday it was! We started in San Francisco, and we went to China Town, and to The Wharf for some local cuisine, which was a huge boiled giant crab, and we went up and down on their local trams.

We hired out some bikes and cycled across the famous Golden Gate Bridge, and at the other end we hired a boat, and stopped off at the notorious Alcatraz Prison Island, before they took us back to the other side. The whole place was amazing, and still to this day, I say San Francisco is my most favourite place in the USA.

Next stop was Las Vegas. For some people who don't know, it's in a desert. I had problems there as it's so dry and all the electric things like slot machines, gave me electric shocks, as I am a very static person.

It was causing havoc with my heart and making me jump everywhere and making me so uncomfortable. Apart from that, what a great place it is. There are helicopters down the Grand Canyon, shows, nightclubs. Even Britney Spears and Justin Timberlake were in the nightclubs. We also had a great stay at the Luxor Hotel; a pyramid hotel with a light on the top of it which shines upwards into Space.

Next stop Los Angeles. Well, this is really the place of Hollywood. We stayed in a beautiful place close to the beach and we went to some lovely restaurants, and the beach where they filmed the famous show Baywatch, that starred David Hasselhoff and the babe Pamela Anderson. We also went to see the basketball courts, where they filmed the great movie *White Men Can't Jump* starring Woody Harrelson, and what a great movie that was.

We went partying with a load of Richard Branson girls from Virgin Airlines, as they were staying in our hotel for their overnight break. We had a right good time with them,

I could have pulled one of them, but I thought as soon as I returned to the UK, I would be back with my girlfriend, as she would have missed me. So instead, I just had a good laugh with this girl as a friend, but she was super fit.

The holiday went super quick and we had an amazing time, but now, we were heading back over the Atlantic to the UK.

When I got back. I texted my girlfriend to let her know I was back, and to see if we could get back together, and she told me that wasn't what she wanted. I thought she might need a bit more time, so I decided to leave it a little longer.

One morning outside my cottage, I was valeting a car for a customer, when I heard the roar of an engine coming. I know my cars, and I know my best mate, the one who sells cars. He had a Ferrari, and I thought it must be his, as he lived not too far down the road. When I looked up, there he was, in his red Ferrari convertible with the top down, and my girlfriend sitting in the passenger seat.

I was heartbroken, and I just didn't want to be anywhere near them or see them together. I loved this area and my cottage and life as it was, but this was too much for me.

I tried to keep out of their way as much as I could, but it was hard because he lived nearby. I tried to get on with life. There was nothing else I could do.

Many great moments and memories with Mini Me on our quad bikes

These were some of the great moments of my life in South America. This photo is at the Panama Canal.

In Morocco going on a 15 hour gruelling road trip to the Atlas Mountains.

Myself in my motorhome touring Europe.

These were some of my best days in and off the Rock of Gibraltar.

My beloved British Bulldog Boss

Many lovely holidays while in Cuba

Sitting on my terrace at home, with my beloved dog Titch, in Malaga, Spain.

Me and my Mum, my world

Me and Mini Me in Tenerife

My skiing trips to Switzerland

CHAPTER FOURTEEN

One day, I was invited to the reception of two friends that had just got married. It was quite a while after my split up with the ex, and I was now over it, and hoping to meet somebody new. The reception was to be held at the Hilton Hotel near Watford, next door to the Old Game Bird pub where I used to go raving many years before. It was going to be a big party, and I don't like to drink and drive, so I booked a night at the hotel.

One of the newly married couple used to live in Canada before moving to the UK, so I knew there would be loads of people from Canada at the reception, and I looked forward to meeting them.

The party was great and what a lovely couple they were. And I kept looking at this one girl that I was attracted to, and she was looking at me. Eventually, I asked her for a dance and gave her some of my Lloyd of the Dance moves. She thought it was so funny and loved dancing with me. We were flirting with each other, and fortunately, she also was staying the night at the hotel. She was Canadian and that night she stayed with me in my room, and we really enjoyed each other's company. She still had another week in the UK, so things were looking good there too, as it would give me time to get to know her better.

Over the next few days, she came and stayed with me at Wrighty's Cottage, and she loved my dog Boss. We went on some lovely walks together and went down the local. It was summertime and I had just bought a nice little Mercedes convertible to sell on. We took it out for a spin to London, so that I could show her the sights. We listened to Frank Sinatra, with both of us singing Mac the Knife. We ended up in Oxford Street for shopping and had a nice meal. She really did love London, and we were having a great time together.

We knew we lived very far away from one another, but it just didn't bother us, as we were having such an amazing time together. Her mum and dad were in the UK as well, and they were really nice people, who were both high ranking Toronto police officers. She told me that she was going to follow in their footsteps and join the force too, one day.

The week went really quickly, and we didn't want it to end, as we were having so much fun, and we were both sad when she had to return to Canada. I was invited to go over there and stay for as long as I wanted. I was so happy I got asked, and I accepted the invitation. That was the beginning of our long-distance relationship, and it was the start of many changes for me, which was just what I needed at that time. A month had passed, and I was ready to go. I had my tickets with Air Canada, and I knew the company very well, as I had clocked up many airmiles with them, and they truly are a nice airline to fly with.

The first time I arrived in Canada, she was too busy to come and pick me up, which I knew anyway, so she sent her brother to come and get me. She told him to take me out to see some sights and make me feel welcome. It was great to see him, and the first place he took me to, was a massive strip club in Toronto. We could have stayed longer, but we didn't take the piss, and instead we cut our fun short, and headed back to her home.

It was great to see her as we hadn't seen each other for a month. We just clicked straight away again. She had prepared lots of food and drinks, as she was hosting a little welcome party for me, so that she could introduce me to her friends. We all enjoyed ourselves, and they all loved my London accent.

Back in the UK she had promised to take me to Niagara Falls, so that was first on the list and she had booked a hotel there too. The next day we went there, and WOW it truly was amazing how big the falls really are. I was so happy to see it, and what a lovely hotel! The next few days we relaxed by these massive lakes, sunbathing and swimming and going nightclubbing and to restaurants in the evenings.

She actually lived in Ontario in a place called Bradford, which was a really nice area. I was enjoying my time in Canada, and once I returned to the UK, we continued with our relationship. I was back and forth from the UK to Canada quite a lot, combining this with seeing my kids, trying to run my home, and doing my work. I also made sure I spent time with my beloved dog, who my mum would look after every time I went away.

Overall, it really was quite tiring and working out very expensive for us both, but I wasn't ready to move over there. I knew she didn't want to live in the UK, and a long-distance relationship did take a toll on us both. It was a shame really, but it was great times, and I am glad we met, and we are still friends today, but it did end our relationship. It was just too far, and I couldn't see myself living there, so we called it a day. After that ended, I thought I was back in the UK for good.

I had only been back for about two weeks and already I just felt unhappy. I had bumped into my ex and the so-called best mate a few times, but I felt I didn't really want to live in the UK anymore. I'd always wanted to live abroad, somewhere like the South of France. I knew I could have probably stayed in Canada, but it was just so far for me and my family. I wanted to be in a hot country where I could start a new life, and Canada had some very cold weather.

I thought it would be a good idea to move into my parents' one bedroomed apartment in the South of Spain. I already knew many people there, and I knew my way around. My kids would be happy too if I lived there, as they would have the best of both worlds, living there and in the UK.

I had already got a dog passport sorted out for Boss, when I was considering the possibility of taking him to

Canada with me. It took me another week to sort out all my things and that was it, I was off in the car with my dog. Happy days. I was looking forward to my new life. Me and the dog got the ferry into France.

Some great friends of mine had retired to Normandy, and they had bought acres of land with a farmhouse on it. I rang them up and said I would like to drop in, and they told me that they were looking forward to seeing me. It was great to see them again, and I ended up staying two nights with them, which was a good rest for me and my dog.

On the first day they took me to visit St Michael, which is a little Island where monks live. The tide comes in and out, and you have to time it right to get to and from the island, if you don't want to get stranded. If the tide came in before your outward journey then you couldn't go anywhere, and if it came in while you were still on the island, you would have to wait until the tide went out again, before you could do the return journey back to the mainland.

On the second day of my stay in Normandy, Bill took me to one of the local bars, while his wife went shopping. Bill loves his Bacardi, and while at the bar he had drunk two whole bottles. His wife returned to pick up both up, and he was smashed. This is the reason he had the nickname the three B's, which stands for, Bill, Bacardi and bed, as obviously his name is Bill, he drinks a lot of Bacardi, and then goes straight to bed.

When I arrived at the Costa del Sol, I was told about the wildfires which had swept through the region a couple of years earlier. The area that suffered the most was Mijas, where there had been fatalities and loss of homes. According to the newspapers, a man had gone missing during this time, and now as I arrived there, they had found a body, but they had absolutely no idea of how he had died. The man was retired and on holiday with his wife. His hobbies were swimming and snorkelling. On the day of the fires, he was swimming off the coastline of Fuengirola, and unaware of the wildfires.

Sea planes and helicopters had been called in to dump water on the fires, and the area was said to be in a state of emergency. Helicopters dangled huge buckets over the sea and plunged for water, which they were then going to dump on the wildfire. Unfortunately, in the process, the man was hoisted up in the bucket with the water, and was then dumped on the burning mountain. The people in the helicopter were completely unaware of what had happened. It was a mountain climber who came across skeletal human remains and alerted people to the man's death.

At the time the newspapers had believed the man must have drowned or been subjected to a shark attack. They would have probably been shocked to know that it was the firefighting efforts of the emergency services, during the wildfires, which had swept him out of the sea, and unceremoniously dumped him into the heart of the fire. Also, back then there was a great white shark, which had supposedly been spotted off the coast of Malaga and was then seen near Sotogrande around that time.

I started to settle in quickly, and enjoyed playing golf on the two courses, and going to the little bar beneath my apartment, where I made many friends. I also frequented the Match room at weekends where there were full size snooker tables. There was also the Byblos Hotel, which is now closed. Rumour had it then that some Japanese businessmen were interested in buying it.

Another place I went to was El Golf restaurant. It was run by a dear friend of mine named Antonio. He and his family were lovely people. I would also go to the Tunisia Hotel, which was owned by a Scottish friend of mine.

Fuengirola was close to where I lived, and it had a sandy beach which was joined with Los Boliches. Nearby are plenty of great restaurants, including traditional Spanish Tapas bars. There are also British bars as well. Fish Alley is off the back street of the beachfront and has plenty of bars and restaurants too. Church Square has an assortment of designer clothes shops, and at the far end of the beach is The Castle. This is the place where they once held Ministry of Sound events. And along the seafront there are many hotels, such as Las Pyramids, and PYR as well as others.

I would go and drink down at the seafront, and I went into the Only Fools and Horses Bar, and the Scots & Irish bar. There were others, like The Three Lions Bar, and the famous London Bar on the corner. There were bars at Fuengirola Marina, where they used to run a market, but they moved them to the Ferrier Ground.

There was plenty of choice, as there was Tramps Bar, Hollywood's, and Lineker's Bar, but I still say that Lineker's Bar was better when it was at the Marina, before they moved it behind the London Bar. Back then, the area was very lively with plenty of nightclubs, such as Heaven's Gate and Undergrounds. These places were really good, and great for dancing the night away. Also, near to where I lived, were places like La Calla, Calahonda, Riviera, La Chapas, Benalmadena, Torremolinos, and Malaga Airport.

The rich and famous were in areas such as Puerto Buenos, and some of the biggest villains in Europe were living alongside them. The people who lived there had flash boats and the most expensive cars.

On the coastline there are many brass houses called clubs, where an escort can be hired. They all live together in massive hotels, which have bars and music. The girls wander around naked, and you can just go in and have a drink and chill out. If you wish, you can pay and go upstairs with one of the girls and do whatever you desire.

One escort place called Estarks 92, which is between Fuengirola and Benalmadena, is a huge hotel with over one hundred girls from all over the world. I've been in there on a few occasions, to meet friends for a drink and have a look at the girls. The girls there are super fit, and many are from South America, Russia, Bulgaria, Romania, and Latvia. You can select a girl, by hair colour, eye colour, and body shape and there is someone for everyone's taste. Other good escort places are Scandalos in Malaga, and the Glass Palace on the way to Estapona, or Selector in Benalmadena.

On a clear day you can see the Rock of Gibraltar, and even Morocco across the Mediterranean if the weather is particularly good. It was such a warm, glowing, beautiful place to live, and I was really enjoying it. I now thought of it as my home, and didn't even think about the UK, with its grey skies, cold rainy weather, and the rat race.

CHAPTER FIFTEEN

I was looking forward to my kids coming over to stay. There were always lots of things to occupy them, such as swimming in the communal swimming pool, or going to the beach in the evening. When they visited, we would go to restaurants.

One of my favourites is called Valparaiso, and it's about halfway up the Mijas Mountain road. As soon as you arrive there, they open your doors for you, and you are shown into a starter room, which is called The Gallery. This is where you get a drink and relax and look at the photos they have on the walls, of the rich and famous who have dined there. I've seen photos there of the Beckhams, as well as famous tennis players, jockey Willie Carson and boxers such as Frank Bruno. The place is popular with those from the entertainment sector and a few old-school crooks.

Once you finish your drink, they take you to your table, and the views are marvellous. You can see the Mediterranean and Fuengirola all lit up in the evenings. Their menu is fabulous. One of my favourites is pink ostrich steak.

While you are there you can listen to the resident singers, singing Frank Sinatra and Pavarotti numbers. I loved it there and I got to know the owners and their sons very well. They would always sort me out a top table, whether I was with my family, with a hot date, or even a bunch of the lads.

I went to many great places like El Oceaner, which is a first-class hotel and restaurant on the beachfront of La Cala. It has sea views, fantastic food and wine, and entertainment. This place is where Ronnie Knight hung out with Barbara Windsor, and there were many other villains who went there, as well as plenty of celebrities.

As nice as the Costa del Sol is, it's got a dark side, and is known by some as the Costa del Crime. This is because it's a gateway to Europe, for smugglers from South America, and Northern Africa. Spain is the capital trade route for the rest of Europe including the UK and has been for many years. Many villains have set up here from all over the world, so that they can run their empires undisturbed.

There are plenty of them, such as the English, the Russians, the Moroccan Cartel, the Turks, old school Yugoslavians, Italian Mafia, Mexicans and Colombians, and they live like kings. They are all fighting amongst themselves for a piece of the action, and it ends up seeming like the board game Monopoly, with so many players.

Not that long ago, there were hitman style shootings in broad daylight. The shooters turned up on fast motorbikes, and just let loose with their guns, having no consideration for innocent people who were dining out or having a drink.

Down at the famous Nikki Beach Bar, there was a similar incident when somebody pulled a gun out and started firing. I was also told a story about the Russians taking a man out to sea off the coast of Marbella, and pushing him off the boat, with heavy weights tied to him.

The place is dangerous and corrupt, and I have heard of the police being paid off to turn a blind eye. Also, if you are pulled as a drink driver, they will let you off if you give them 500 Euros. I know a bloke whose friend is a bit of a player, and we were in the Only Fools and Horses one day when he turned up. He told my friend that he came through the airport with £70,000, and when he got stopped by the police, they told him that he could either get nicked, or walk away with half of the money. He immediately gave half of the money to them, and then the police left him alone. Obviously, he was pissed off, but it was the lesser of two evils.

He hurried outside in case they suddenly changed their minds and asked for more. Then, as he reached the car that was waiting for him, he saw the same two officers racing towards him. He thought they were either going to demand more money or nick him, but all they wanted him for was to return the passport they'd taken to check his details!

Also, on the Costa (the coast), you always hear of speed boats pulling up to the beaches, and unloading their stash for 4-wheel drive cars. It's easier for them to have it driven off across the sand, but sometimes they lose their stuff if the cars don't get there quickly enough, as it gets washed up on the beaches, where dog walkers or tourists find it, and call the police.

I was living here for some time, and I was lucky I didn't have to pay rent. I was getting money from the rental of my cottage back home, but I was hammering the drink and just lying around the pool all day, and the beach. I was getting bored, and I wanted a job to give me something to do, as well as earning myself a bit of money.

I had just bought a quad bike and I also had my son's quad bike shipped over. He and I had some wicked times riding up Mijas Mountain. I would always be up at the front, checking that the route we were taking was safe and clear.

One time, when I looked around to make sure that he was still behind me, I couldn't see him. My heart was pumping with fear. I quickly backtracked. When I heard him shouting for help, I went towards the sound of his voice and realised he had ridden the bike off the edge. Luckily for him, the quad bike got wedged on a rock, or he would have gone straight down over the edge and might have died.

I climbed down to him and brought him back up, and understandably, he was shaking like a leaf. I comforted him, then I went back down there with a tow rope attached to my quad bike, which I then tied to his bike. I started my quad up and was able to drag my son's bike back up, but it was very scary. It was a long time before my son went on the quad again, and I don't blame him.

My mate Lee from Watford, who also lived in Spain, was selling designer flip flops and was making a killing, so I wanted a piece of the action. I bought a hundred pairs a time off him, and I would get on my quad bike, and go up and down the beach fronts selling them. The tourists bought plenty of them, and I also sold them in a few bars, such as Andy's Beach Bar.

One day when I was in Fuengirola, selling flip flops, I took a break and sat down on a beach chair to have a drink and sunbathe. I started to chat to a man nearby, and as I went to leave, he said, 'Oi mate, you've got a bit of shit on your back.'

I bent my arm to try to wipe it off, thinking the chair must have been dirty, and he started laughing. He then pointed out that he was talking about my Chelsea tattoo, the cheeky fucker. It did make me laugh though.

I wanted to do something else to bring in more money, so I put an advert in the local paper, to say that I did a service collecting cars from the UK and bringing them to Spain. I thought it was a good idea, as not everybody who is relocating wants to drive that long distance.

Over the years I had a few calls. Once I picked up a top of the range Mustang from the UK and really enjoyed the drive down. Usually, I wouldn't bother driving through France. Instead, I would get the ferry from Plymouth or Portsmouth. Once I got there, I would have a night out and stay overnight at a hotel.

Once I got off the ferry, I would drive from Bilbao or Santander, then all the way down to Malaga, and it paid very well. I was always on the lookout for things that could make money for me, and this was just one more string to my bow. I was living a very nice life, and I was actually enjoying the work I was doing, because I was my own boss.

Not only that, but there was the nightlife, the nice weather, and the fact that I was on the beach every day. It was vastly different to the life I had been leading in the UK. When I was selling the flip flops, it was the ideal job for me, as I am very sociable, and I really enjoyed talking to the tourists and getting to know them.

It had been a long summer. I'd had the kids over, and I had done all I wanted to do with work. Now, it was time for me to really enjoy myself.

CHAPTER SIXTEEN

I decided to take a trip to Thailand. The first stop was Turkey, and fortunately, I had a friend there. I'm lucky in that I have friends all over the world. It certainly comes in handy when you are unfamiliar with a place, and you need somebody to show you around, or you need somewhere to stay, while you are on your travels.

Back in Spain, a friend of mine was a property investor, who I'd picked up a few cars for, and now he had invested in some property in Bodrum in Turkey. He asked me to look over some of his investment properties, and sort out some furniture for them, as he knew I had good taste in interior design. I jumped at the chance, as it would be a good stopover, before my onward flight to Thailand.

During the time I was in Bodrum, I was busy overseeing the properties and sorting them out. They were nice three bedroomed villas with pools, right by the sea, looking out towards the smaller Greek island, which is known as Kos.

I knew Kos very well, and it brought back bad memories. The first time I went there was when my mum and stepdad took me. I was playing in the hotel pool, and a big black beetle went into my swimming trunks, and its pincers bit my ball sac. My mum had to help remove it from me, while I was crying my eyes out. It really was a horrible, painful experience, and I was lucky it wasn't a poisonous one.

The second time I visited Kos, was even worse. I was away on a lad's holiday. It was my birthday, and while we were there, we all rented scooters. I got into a crash when a car came straight at me, and I went over the top of it and ended up in hospital. I knocked some of my teeth out, and needed stitches, but I was lucky to be alive.

At the time I said I was never going back there again, but here I was once again, having a stopover before going on to Thailand. I just hoped that no more bad luck would come my way.

When I arrived in Thailand I was buzzing. I had two nights in Bangkok, before my next flight onto Koi Samui.

The first thing on my mind was the food, as I think Asian food is the best in the world. I like Indian meals, Chinese meals, and a bit of Filipino food, which is spicier than Thai, but Thai is my number one favourite. After dinner I took the tuk-tuk bike down to where all the lively go-go bars were, as well as massage parlours and discos.

My next stop was a nice massage. I found a nice little place, and you always get the opportunity to have more than just a massage. All you need to do is to ask for a happy ending, or they ask you if you want it. It's a crazy, wild, but lovely place. After my massage I felt like a new man, and my food had gone down a treat.

Now, I was fit and ready to hit the disco, and throw a few moves on the dance floor. I was looking forward to giving it some of the LOTD moves and shapes. I found this great pumping, open rooftop bar. The music was a bit of hardcore and trance, and there were great laser lights. It was nice looking out to the sky and seeing the stars. I grabbed myself a bottle of Chag which is Thai local beer, and I hit the dancefloor.

After about ten minutes of dancing, a girl approached me, and at first, I didn't recognise her.

'Lloydie boy (LOTD) is it you?' I still didn't really know who it was. Then she said, 'It's Kim, you nutter, from secondary school.'

I was really shocked but it was great to see her. We had a laugh and a dance, and we thought it was so funny, meeting up like that. We had a quick kiss and cuddle, wished each other a great holiday and said our goodbyes.

After two days in Bangkok, I got my flight to Koi Samui, where I relaxed for a few days, before the big party on Ko Phangan, which is where they have the famous Full Moon Party. I visited a buddha temple and relaxed in a few bars and on the beach.

I decided to go for a swim, even though I'm not a strong swimmer, but once I was in the sea, I found I was struggling to get back to the shore. The undercurrent flows were making me drift, and I started to panic. I tried my hardest and pushed myself to the limit, and thankfully I finally made it ashore, where I collapsed with exhaustion.

To my surprise when I looked up, I didn't recognise the part of the beach I was on. I started to walk back up the beach to my right, to look for my beach towel. To my shock and horror, it must have been a good mile, before I got where I wanted to go, as the dangerous current had taken me that far.

I went to the Full Moon Party after I arrived on the island by boat, which was laid on to ferry people back and forth. People come here from all over the world for this event, which is held along the beaches, with the full moon coming up over the sea, and the bars pumping out loud hardcore techno music, with lights and lasers everywhere. There were thousands of weird and wonderful people, dancing and getting off their tits and head, and going crazy to the music and jumping over beach fires. It really was a huge super party, and it went on until the next day.

The following day, I missed the boat which had been laid on, as I was still drinking and was off my head. I ended up on the way back, paying this local fisherman to take me back in his boat. I sat there tangled up in smelly fishing nets, and when I got back to the hotel, I must have stunk of fish. I went straight to my room to recover from the party, which I truly enjoyed, and would recommend to anyone who wants to let their hair down.

Sadly, my time in Thailand ended, and I returned to Spain, but things weren't right with me. I had something on my mind, which was really bugging me and eating me up inside.

I had been back in Spain for a few months, and in the next month or so I was going to the UK to see my kids for a few days, but the thing on my mind was worrying me immensely.

During my stay in Thailand, I met a Thai girl. And it was a girl, not a ladyboy or transvestite, as you have to be so careful out there. We liked one another and had sex on a number of occasions, but the condom had split and come off inside her a couple of times. It was making me ill with worry, thinking about it. I decided to get checked out while I was in the UK.

I went to Luton hospital to have blood tests at the GUM clinic, and I had other tests as well to make sure I didn't have HIV, or other things, and they said they would contact me if there was a problem. I told them I lived in Spain, and I gave them my Spanish mobile number, and they told me it would take two weeks for the tests to come back.

Those two weeks really dragged, and I was worrying like mad. I couldn't keep still or rest or sleep properly until the two weeks were up.

CHAPTER SEVENTEEN

There was only two days left of the two weeks that the Luton GUM clinic said they would call, and I was on edge. At this point in time, a friend of mine was over in the UK doing some work for me, picking a car up, to bring it down to Spain for me and my client.

On this particular day, I was relaxing by the swimming pool, and I dozed off. I was woken up by my phone ringing, and when I looked down at the screen, I saw that it was a Luton code number of 01582.

I shit myself, and started to shake, and I felt sick, thinking this is it. It's the hospital, telling me I have caught something. It took me longer than usual to answer the call, as I was really shitting it. I pressed the answer button.

To my surprise, I heard, 'Lloydie boy, it's me. All is okay with me and the car. I am just stopping for a drink and getting some petrol.'

It was my mate who was picking the car up in the UK from up North, and he was just pulling in for a pitstop, of all places at Luton, and he was using the phone box to call me from.

I just couldn't quite believe it, and I started swearing at him, 'You wanker, what are you doing to me?'

He was puzzled until I explained to him about who I had thought was on the other end of the phone. He understood then why I was so stressed out, but it really did put the wind up me. Even after that phone call, I was still shaken up by it. Talk about timing and places, I thought.

After that call there was no call from the clinic and thank God for that. My worries were now gone.

Back on the coast here, I was enjoying my life, and my kids loved coming back and forth. I had made so many friends, not just English, but people from all over the world. Things were going well, and life was sweet. In my spare time, I loved to play a round of golf on one of the many golf courses, which are up and down the coastline.

I remember one of my favourite courses called Rio Real. This course is on the way down to Marbella. It's one of the most expensive places to play. It really is an elite golf course, with such wonderful, beautiful views. It stretches right down to the blue Mediterranean beach line.

On this one occasion, I was playing, and I was just about to tee off, which means you are just about to hit the ball with your golf club. Before I could do this, I was distracted, as there was a noise coming from behind me. I could see a golf buggy coming towards me, and I could hear some music coming from it, so that put me off. The next thing I saw could have been out of a James Bond movie.

There was this customised golf buggy, which had alloy wheels. It was petrol with road number plates on the front and back. It had a car stereo, which was where the music was coming from. There was a champagne holder with the bottle in it, a mini fridge, and on the back of the buggy was a golf set, made out of gold and shining in the reflection of the sun. It was just gleaming. In the golf buggy was this old smart guy, and next to him was this young super fit model, with a huge boob job. She really was beautiful, first class totty. I thought to myself, wow, talk about money and power, and what a way to play golf!

I decided to watch him play, instead of teeing off, so I let him go in front, as I didn't want to hit my ball in front of them, in case I did a shit shot. They thanked me, and went through, and as they went off into the distance, I thought, who the fuck was that?

I remember on another occasion, I was playing golf on a course up near the airport in Malaga, El Parador, and it was so funny. I was playing golf with one of my best mates called Norm, and he hit this mega shot, which went over the fence, off the golf course, and onto the beach.

As we were getting closer to where he had hit the ball, to our surprise we saw this bum going up and down in the air. We both thought jackpot! Look there's two people right at it, having sex on the beach. Let's get closer. We could see our ball quite close to them, and at this point we were unaware what kind of beach this was.

We got close to the fence, then we whistled and shouted that we were coming to get our ball. To our shock, they both got up and it was two blokes fucking away. They picked our ball up and threw it over to us, and we were gobsmacked. We stood there thinking, *dirty little fuckers.* We got more balls out of our golf bags, and started throwing them at them as they were running off down the beach. It was so funny.

Apart from playing golf, I spent a lot of my time where I lived on Mijas, where I had lots of close friends. There was John and Lyn, Tony and Wendy, Chris and Hitch, and there was Justin and Nikki, and another Tony who has now died of cancer. Also, there was Harry and Pete, and Jan, and the Spanish man Harrado, who owned the local bar. They are all very close friends to me, and Nikki is like a sister to me.

I had lots more friends too, and it really was a great place to live. There were many older people who lived on Mijas Golf too, and they didn't drive anymore, because of their age and medical problems, like Harry and Peter.

Every week I would pick them up and take them out to lunch, and to get their weekly shopping, and we would go for a few cheeky beers. They were great friends of mine, and I loved to look after them, and I got a great deal of satisfaction from helping them. It all came from my heart, and the way my mum brought me up, as she was such a wonderful mother.

My mate Justin, and his dad were from Jersey, and they had lived on Mijas for many years before I came. They owned a couple of places and were very wealthy people. Justin's dad was hard and was not a loving man, and he had lost his mother a long time before. He became a good friend of mine, but there was always something missing from him. I'm sure it was love and care.

A little time afterwards, Justin's dad died, and he left him nearly a million pounds and both of the properties, so he became a rich man, but there was always this one thing missing for him, which was love. He had a little drug problem too, but it wasn't like he was an addict, he just liked to party. On many occasions, me and him would hit the coast on nights out, dancing, and getting drunk and out of our heads.

One night, we were introduced to the fanny club in between Fuengirola and Benalmadena. This is where he met the love of his life, Fabiana. She was a fit Brazilian girl who worked there.

I told him that beautiful as she was, she was a working girl and all she saw was money, but he couldn't see past the lust, and the sex that she was giving him. She was telling him that she loved him, but she was still working at the club. He was infatuated with her, and would do anything for her. He gave her lots of money, dinners out and shopping trips, because for him it was love.

As I said, he never really had love in his life, but since he'd met her, he thought his life was now filled with love and she was the best thing ever. They had been dating for a while, and he was head over heels in love, but she still continued to work at the club.

He told me that she said that when she stopped working there, she wanted him to move to Brazil with her, to start a family, and a business there for them all. He said that he was going to sell one of his properties and would leave one under the control of our mutual good friends, Nikki and Tony, so that they could rent it out for him. He told me that he had decided to go to Brazil, to buy some places, and set up a business.

I told him that he was mad, and warned him to be careful, but he could see nothing else but love, so I wished him the best of luck with following his heart, and that is what he did.

He moved to Brazil and bought a few apartments, and two kid's clothing shops. Things were looking good for them, but his girlfriend had a coke problem, and was out scoring off her dealer all the time. She got pregnant from her dealer but turned around and told Justin the baby was his, and he was over the moon.

A few months down the line, he discovered it wasn't his and that it was the dealer's baby, but he still stood by her, and said he would be the father to this baby that was going to be born. But after a few months passed, she left him for the same dealer, but what happened next, was even worse.

All of Justin's properties were in his girlfriend's name, and he lost the lot. Most of all his heart had been broken, and he didn't have much money left, as she had spent it all. This was such a shame and shouldn't have happened to such a nice fellow.

I have since heard that to get by for a living, he sells crack for the gangs out at the Flava's, to all the tourists who are there on holiday. From what I hear, he is at rock bottom, with a craving for drugs himself, but I did warn him.

I had been single for quite a while, and I was just having fun, but I had my eye on this fit girl who worked in one of the internet shops, the ones you can make cheap calls from. At the time, I didn't know that she was also a lap dancer in the evenings, and I was interested in getting to know her better. We got on very well and I became really fond of her, and soon we were going out.

She had a great tattoo of Tweetie Pie on her arse cheeks, which was great too. We started going out for drinks and food, and I took her to the famous Valparisso, up on the Mijas road, and to other top restaurants up and down the coast.

After a while, I found out she was a lap dancer, and I thought fair play, as she had a nice, cute arse, and nice firm tits. In my eyes she was making money from her assets, and we were getting on quite well.

I booked us a trip to Cuba, and what a great trip it was. I booked a beautiful all-inclusive hotel in the resort Varadero which has great white sandy beaches, and plenty of venues to enjoy. There were also some good golf courses where I could play.

It truly was a delightful place. While we were there we came across this lake, and also a restaurant dug into side of the cave which was next to the lake. It really was an amazing place, with top food. Proper class.

While we were staying in Cuba, I booked an overnight stay in Havana. When we got there, we saw all the old classic cars, and little old ladies smoking fat cigars, sitting on doorsteps, in the old town area. The vibes were great, with Latina music, Salsa, pumping out of windows in the alleyways. It really is a place that buzzes, and the people are ever so friendly.

During our stay there, we went to see the famous Havana cigar factory, and saw them rolling the leaves and making the cigars. Another trip was to the Rum factory, where I nicked a bottle of Rum, and bought one and got pissed out of my head, which my girlfriend wasn't too pleased about. I was pissing off all the Germans on the coach, being loud, but I was oblivious to it, as I had been drinking, and I was just enjoying myself.

Our stay in Cuba was really a great time, and as we left, I promised myself I would be back one day for more.

CHAPTER EIGHTEEN

Back in Spain, I was meeting and making new friends, and some were in the drug game, and some were not. You either came to Spain retired, or you came young to work in bars or restaurants. If you were really lucky, you would set up your own legit business, and fingers crossed, you would do well.

Spain can be a tough place to find a good paid job. Some people come out for two or three years with a load of savings, and just blow the lot on the piss, and lying about in the sun, doing fuck all. Then they go back to Blighty with not a pot to piss in.

For me, things were good. I used to like going on shopping trips up in Malaga to Plazor Mayor, and the big El Corte Ingles. And back in Fuengirola, they had just built a massive new shopping mall, which was called the Miri Mar. In here they had built a twelve screen cinema complex, where they would play three or four screens in English to accommodate the tourists and the many expats that lived there. There was also a great big skateboard park.

Things were changing for the better in this area, and they even opened up a British Iceland supermarket. This was great for the expats, and for me too, as before it opened, we would all take the long trip down to Gibraltar, to go shopping at Morrison's and Marks and Sparks. They also had a go cart track, and the hippodrome where they did live horse racing events, which were truly top days out.

They did night racing in the summer months, as it was so hot. You could put on a bet and watch the race and go in one of the many bars around the track, with live music and great restaurants. I had many great nights and days here with my kids.

I also joined the Fuengirola darts league and played for many bars over a ten-year period. Because I was known as L.O.T.D. Lloyd of the Darts, when I was playing darts, I was called out every Tuesday, playing in all the bars up and around Fuengirola. They were great times, and I got to meet so many nice people.

When the kids came over for holidays, I liked to take them to different areas. We would have a week up in Neja, or go down to Tarifa, and even one Xmas we stayed down in Gibraltar in the Calata Hotel. The views are amazing, looking over to Morocco in South Africa.

Another good thing was at Malaga Airport, Fly Monarch was doing daily flights from Luton to Spain every day of the week, so me and my family joined the Monarch club, and because of the flights, I was building up airmiles, going back and forth, and I became a gold card member. This helped because if I wanted to change a flight, it would be free of charge. I could choose my seat, and with extra legroom, and have extra weight on my cases. You had a VIP area in Malaga and Luton Airport for refreshments, so it was great. On the other occasions, I would fly with EasyJet. Sadly, Fly Monarch has finished, which is a shame as it was such a great company. Over the years I knew many of the staff and became good friends with them. I was sad to see them go. On other occasions, I would fly from Stansted with Ryanair too, as that was good for extra options.

Over a period of years, my mum would fly over to see me, but in the last few years she was becoming unwell, and if she flew, her legs would swell up, and she always had bad asthma with breathing problems, so she decided not to fly any longer.

Instead, she took her time with my stepdad, and would drive down to Spain to see us. I noticed that back at home she was hardly going out anywhere and I was starting to worry and think about her a lot, as I am a mummy's boy. I love her so much and she's done so much for me, and she is an amazing person.

When she came to visit, her main interest which she enjoyed was up in the mountains where the little Mijas village is. She enjoyed the amazing views and how Spanish it was away from the coastline and all the tourists. She loved the old Bullring up there, and the way life, and the old-fashioned donkeys walking about.

She really did love this place, but like I said, back at home she was hardly going out. I noticed she couldn't get far without getting out of breath, so every time I was in the UK to see my kids, I would stay with her to keep an eye out.

On one of the trips I'd had my Wrighty's Cottage up for sale and I had sold it. This was exciting as I had just put a deposit down on a new bigger place for us all, in the neighbouring La Cala hills, which is at the back end of Mijas Golf. So, with Wrighty's Cottage sold, we could move on, and like I said, it's bigger, so the kids had their own rooms.

This place was really first class. It had two big swimming pools, a 24-hour security gated entrance, the most beautiful views to the sea, and beautiful views to Mijas Mountain. And I had underneath garage parking. To me this was my point of staying for good, as my cottage was sold, and I had nothing left in the UK now. I had already lived in Spain for over 4 years now, so to me Spain was my future life. I had my own home which I loved, and the kids did as well.

I also had my British Bulldog Boss when I moved in, but he had this lump growing over his eye. At first, it didn't look very nice, and the other thing I thought was that it would start to upset him. When it grew bigger, I took him to the vets to see what they said, or what they could do for him. They did some tests which all came back clear, but they said that the lump would get bigger and would stop him from seeing out of that eye. They said the best thing for him would be a simple operation to remove it, and to make sure it didn't grow back again.

After a month or so, it didn't stop growing, so the only option was to remove it, so I booked him in for the operation, and I rang the kids and told my mum about it, as they loved him so much.

On the day of the op, the vets told me to drop him off in the morning, then come back in the afternoon to pick him up, so that's what I did. I gave him massive cuddles and kisses, and then dropped him off and left him, and went to the beach to try and relax. Even though they had said it's just a normal little operation, and nothing to worry about, to me, he was my baby and I had done so much with him. We had spent over 5 years of our lives together, so he was my best friend too, so I just couldn't relax until I saw him and picked him up.

The whole morning went at a snail's pace, and I was so anxious until the time came to get him. Finally, I was back at the vets to pick my boy up. While I waited the vet came to greet me, and said the operation had gone well, and he had removed the fatty tissue away, and Boss was still a little dozy, but coming around after the op. He suggested that we did the paperwork, so I paid him for the operation, then he said I should go for a coffee, and come back in half an hour to pick him up.

When I came back and saw him, I could see where they had removed the lump, and they had done a good job, but he was still out of it. The vet said it was okay to take him home and let him rest but said that I should keep an eye on him.

I picked him up and took him to my car. His eyes were open, and I knew he knew I was with him and that he could hear me. I was telling him it was okay and that it was all over now, but to me he just didn't look right. I just thought it was because of the op he had just been through, and that's why he was so sleepy. I took it easy and got him home as quickly as possible, and carried him into the front room, and laid him on his big bed on the floor, in front of the TV, which I put on to comfort him. I sat with him for a while on the floor, giving him some rubs, and talking to him like a crazy man, thinking he's going to reply.

After a while of this, I got up and went to my sofa to lay down too, and keep an eye on him, as I was now tired. I fell asleep, but after about an hour I woke up and looked straight down to where he was, and I noticed he had moved himself around on his bed, and I couldn't see his face. I noticed bless him, that he'd weed himself, and shit himself, so I jumped up, just thinking *poor fucker, he can't help it because of what he's been through.* I went over to see him and clean him up, and when I got close, I could see he wasn't breathing. I looked at his face in horror, and his tongue was right out, and his mouth was lockjaw. I shouted, 'Boss, nooooo, please don't go,' and I tried to open his mouth and blow down it. I pushed his chest with the palm of my hands, trying desperately to get him back to life. I was in a right state myself after a while of trying, as I knew he was dead, and I just fell to the floor, sobbing and thinking *my poor boy, he's gone.*

It took me a while to pull myself together after Boss died. I was really missing him, and was thinking of our times together, and all the years that went past from his puppy days up until that day he went to doggy heaven. What was really hard was the first couple of weeks. I found it hard to go home, as normally when I opened the front door, he would come running to greet me. Sadly, that was there no more, and it was tearing me apart. So, I booked myself into a cheap hostel, and I didn't go home at all for a few days, as it was too much for me. I felt as if somebody had chopped my arms off, and in my head, I could still hear myself calling him, as though he was still there.

When I did finally go home, it felt weird, and too quiet, and I felt so low and lonely. Down on the Fuengirola seafront at the Scotts and Irish bar, I arranged a send-off for him, and everybody came that knew me and Boss. There was Manchester Mark, Rob The Dog, my good pal Gary from London, and many more. It really was a good send off for Boss. After a couple of weeks passed, I still found it hard to go home as I thought I had nothing to go home for. I was starting to drink heavily. Most days I would just stay on the beach, and one day I was there, and it was a really windy day, and they had the colour coded flags out, to warn people that it was dangerous to swim, as you could drown.

The next minute I heard this lady screaming, and pointing to this person in the sea, and you could see that the person was in danger, as he was going underwater, and finding it hard to swim. I heard some whistles, and the lifeguards turned up and jumped into the sea to get him. They were trying so hard to swim out and get him, and they were struggling, and were getting pushed back by the strong waves.

You could just about see the person in trouble now, as he was going under even more, and the guards just couldn't get to him. The next minute, this looky-looky man turned up on the beach, and could see what was going on. He just dropped all the things that he was selling on the beach, and jumped into the sea, and got past the two lifeguards, and reached the man in danger. He grabbed him and brought him back to the beach. Everybody started clapping and whistling. It was totally something else, and we were in awe. As for the gossip that looky-looky men are a pain in the arse, this one was defo not. For sure he had saved this man's life. As for me, time is a healer in life, but my poor dog will never ever be forgotten, and will always be truly missed.

CHAPTER NINETEEN

The girl I was seeing, was more of a friend than a girlfriend, but a friend with benefits. I had arranged for us both to go on a trip to Morocco, so we headed down past Gibraltar, to Tarifa to get the ferry across. I had never been to Morocco before, and this was going to be the first of many trips to this wonderful country.

Like I said earlier, I had spent time in Tunisia before, and once I had a trip to the Gambia, where they say the smiley people live, and what a place that was. I remember it very well, and they have two types of taxis. One is green and one is yellow. The yellow one is like a town taxi, and the green one is like a bush taxi. What is so funny, is that while we were there, me and my girlfriend at the time, flagged down a green one without knowing.

What happened next was hilarious. The taxi just pulled over on the roadside, while me and my girlfriend were in it, and started picking up other people. This lady got in with a chicken, and these two kids. We just started laughing and thought the experience was funny, and when we got back to the hotel, the reception told us that when a green taxi is not full, anyone can jump in and use it, but the yellow ones were for the towns, so they can't stop for anyone else.

Also, while there, I booked us a fishing trip to Banjil, and caught all types of fish, including a Parrot fish. We went around all the river roots of Banjil, until finally we came to the mouth of the river, which looks like the sea, but it's not. It's still the river, but it's seven miles wide. It really is something else to see, and I really loved the Gambia.

But now we were in Morocco. It was great to be heading back onto the African continent. We left Spain from the

Tarifa port, and it was so beautiful to be in the Mediterranean Sea. What happened next should have been something out of a David Attenborough programme.

There were hundreds of dolphins swimming to everywhere the eye could see, and I had never ever seen so many. On other occasions, I had seen them in the Bay of Biscay, on a ferry coming from the UK to Spain, but never as many as I saw then. It truly was remarkable, and it put a tear in my eyes, and a smile on my face, to see nature at its best.

We arrived in Morocco in the port of Tangier. There were people already coming up to us, trying to sell us rugs and touting for a ride in unlicenced taxis. They were also trying to get us to go on trips to other places, but I had already planned for our hotel to send us a taxi of their own.

We were staying at the famous El Minzah hotel up in the top end of the old town, which is really first class. It's an old hotel, which is French Moroccan, and it has three restaurants inside it, a gym, and a spa. It also has a great photo gallery of all the rich and famous who have stayed there, and some of the old motor races with cars and faces from back in the old days, as Morocco held some great car races over the years. We were well happy with what we had booked, but I knew it would be great, as some of my Moroccan friends had told me to stay there, and that I would like it. I was going to meet some of them, while I was in Morocco.

Like I said, back in the UK some of my friends were criminals, and in Spain too, and now I had made and met some Moroccans and some of them were criminals. Two of them were from a well-known family, and were part of the Moroccan cartel, but like I said before, it's up to you what you do. A friend is a friend, so to me that's it.

During our stay there I fell in love with the place and its people, and I loved the hustle and bustle of the old town, and its market, and their food. We also went riding up and down the beachfront on camel back and we were smoking the pipe and drinking tea.

We were really having a good time. I met up with my Moroccan friends, and they were talking about the Moroccan hash that came out of there. I was well surprised how cheap it was there, compared to the cost of Europe. Some people must be making a killing, and of course the Moroccan cartel that were running it. But well, to me, I was just here for my holidays, and like I said I loved the place, and couldn't wait to come back.

Back in Spain, I was still lonely at home without my dog. The only thing I thought of was to get another one. Me and my girlfriend had gone our separate ways. She ended up moving to New Zealand, where her sister had settled.

After a while, I found this lady selling French Bulldogs, and I instantly fell in love with them. I came away with one of them to take home. He was a boy, and I called him after my favourite clothing brand. Yes, I called him AJ from Armani, but also while I was there, I fell in love with these miniature Doberman Pinschers, and one was also a boy, so I bought one of them too. I was so excited and happy to get them home.

The Doberman I named Titch, as he was the smallest, one in the litter. I know Boss only just died a couple of months before, but to me I was sad without a dog. Now I was giving this life and love to two more dogs, and it made me happy. The home didn't feel empty anymore. It wasn't quiet, and I loved being home with the boys, and now I had reasons to go home. I had routine back in my life, but in my heart and memories, Boss will never be forgotten.

Another one of my part-time jobs in Spain, was taking friends and neighbours to the airport. They would either give me some money, or they would take me out for a meal, or when they left, they would give me all of their food out of the fridge, or a few bottles of wine. This always kept me busy in my spare time, or even sometimes, I would work a few hours, here and there in people's bars. I knew every extra bit of money helped. I had lived in Spain for over 7 years now, and you have to do whatever it is to make money. It can be tough sometimes, but I just loved Spain, and I said I never ever wanted to return to grey old Blighty.

There was an old neighbour of mine, who couldn't drive anymore, so he sold me his car on the cheap, and I used it as my second car. Then, more neighbours heard I had a second car, and the ones that didn't live here and just came on holiday, would hire the car off me for the week or two that they were there. Things were good, and that gave me my next plan. I thought of a name and called my new idea Wrightscars2hire.

What I did was I went around a few car-hire places, and got all of their numbers, and spoke with them, and made some business cards up with my name and number, and my business title, and gave them out to all my neighbours, and in the bars up and down the coast. When anybody rang me, I would get them a car, and I would earn my commission on top. So, happy days and sweet as a nut, I thought, as things were going well.

One day I spoke to one of my clients, and he said that the car had been stolen. The car in question was my second car. He said what happened next was that he had only nipped into the supermarket for a couple of items, and he left the keys in the ignition, and thought it would be okay. Then, to his surprise on his return, somebody had taken it. I thought *for fucks sake you idiot, what a prick*.

I rang the insurance people and told them about it, that it had been nicked, but I didn't tell them about the keys being in it, as I knew they wouldn't pay out, and I left it at that. With the insurance people notified, I thought I would leave it there, and was hoping that after a few days, it would pop up somewhere.

Well, it did pop up somewhere! It had been in an armed robbery. It was inland in a place called Coin, and also it had been in a police chase, and it had been damaged, and also shot at by the police. Whoever did the robbery got away, and the police found the keys still in it. Now the police thought I had something to do with it. What a joke, I thought. As if I am going to do an armed robbery in my own car! Are they crazy or what? I was told to go to the police station where the car was, which I did, and luckily for me, I didn't fit the description of the armed robber in the shop, or the getaway driver that the police had seen.

Anyway, I told them the story of what happened, and after that they didn't need to talk to me anymore. They said I could have a quick look at the car, which was in a right mess. It had two bullet holes in the back, and the police said that I couldn't get the car back as it was evidence, and they would be keeping it.

They told me to talk with my insurance company, so I did, but on the police report it said that the keys were in it, and they didn't pay me a penny. But I made the bloke who rented it pay for the car.

CHAPTER TWENTY

It had been a long summer, and I had my kids over for the holidays, and my best friend Norm, who has always been like a brother to me.

He was telling me about my ex best mate, the millionaire car dealer, and I knew already that he had split up with my ex-girlfriend. When he told me who he was with now, and that he'd married her, I couldn't quite believe it. It was only one of my other ex-girlfriends, the one I was going to marry, who had slept with my brother!

I had cancelled the wedding and finished with her of course, but. I thought wow, this bloke defo likes my seconds. What else I thought was quite funny, and that was that she had only just been in contact with me, to meet up, and was telling me that I was the only man she will every properly love and want. It did make me laugh, as I know she was only with him for the money, like the last one, and I thought best of luck, and had a chuckle to myself.

Where I lived, I loved the new place, and the dogs settled in quickly too, and all the neighbours were great, and friendly too, perhaps a little too friendly. I got invited to a BBQ party one hot afternoon by a lovely couple that I had spoken to on many occasions around the swimming pool, and when walking with my dogs. They would always say hello, and stuff. I told them that I would come to the party.

I grabbed a couple of bottles of wine, and headed over there. After a couple of hours, I thought it was strange, as nobody else turned up. It was just us there, and by that point in time, the drinks were flowing, and we were all quite drunk, and in a great mood, just happy and laughing and enjoying ourselves. I went to the toilet, and when I came back, they were at it, having sex, and they asked me to join in. 'Come on, what are you waiting for?' they said

That was my first time at swinging, and it did take me by surprise, but I had to say, it wasn't the last time either. It happened again, but with different neighbours. I blame it on the heat. Me and everybody get freaky and bonkers. It's crazy, but it's all good fun, as long as there is no harm.

As I said, I think it's the heat that attracts people, as even one of my other neighbours was a well-known porn star, named Lynsey Dawn Mackenzie. I became good friends with her, and on one occasion when I was flying to the UK to Luton airport, by chance we got to sit next to one another on the plane, and she offered me a lift in the limo at the other end, but when we landed my mum was already there waiting to pick me up. That was a shame, as maybe I would have become a porn star too. Ha ha!

It had been a long great year, and now it was time to date again. I had been chatting for a while to this girl online. She was a Philippino girl, and I had booked a holiday to go over and see her in the Philippines. I couldn't wait as I love Asia so much. That was it, I was off.

Firstly, I took the bullet train up to Madrid, as I stopped flying to places from the UK, as this was much easier, and I would visit friends for a couple of days in Madrid, before I left. So, all was good, and I headed off on my holidays.

I landed in Manila, with the City right in the middle of a monsoon, and boy when it rains there, it does rain. The place was really bad with flash floods, and it was chaos. I had already arranged for the girl to greet me on my arrival, which she did, so all was fine there.

Then we grabbed a taxi to the hotel I'd booked online. We were staying at Dusit Hotel, right bang in the middle of Manila. I was really pleased to see this girl, and she was to see me. Before this we had only chatted on the net through chat rooms and MSN messenger or webcam, and we had built up a great relationship. We did chat also about what we wanted from a relationship, and the thing we said to each other was that we would be friends at first, and I was just coming over on holiday, to visit her beautiful country, and stay with her and her family, so that I would experience the proper Philippino lifestyle. We said if we did find love together, then we would start a relationship from there.

Well, the first night, I was ever so tired, after all the flying I had done, and I was jetlagged, and this was the furthest I had ever flown before. On the way I did stop over at Abu Dhabi and I had a few hours rest, but I was so shattered, and I told the girl I needed an early night, and a very good sleep, and she said she fully understood. So, I said my good nights and told her I would be fully charged the following day, and then we could start to explore her beautiful country. I had booked a hotel room with two separate rooms, with beds, so she left me and went to her room.

The next morning, I was still fast asleep, and I found I had missed breakfast downstairs, but she had got up and gone for breakfast, and didn't want to wake me after my long travel. While down at the breakfast hall, she picked up a tray and brought it back up to me, with loads of fresh fruit, bread, yoghourt and coffee.

She came to my room with the tray and woke me up and said, 'Good morning Mr Wright, my king. Your breakfast is served,' which I thought was ever so sweet of her, and I thanked her. As I woke up properly and looked around the room, I saw she had unpacked my bag and hung up all my shirts and put all my toiletries in the bathroom, which I said was very sweet of her, and I thanked her.

She spoke good English, but she said that when we went to stay at her house, her parents didn't speak English, but like we spoke before on the net, her parents didn't mind me coming to stay, and welcomed me there, but when talking to me, they would use their daughter to translate. I was ever so excited about staying with a Philippino family for the experience, and I couldn't wait to meet them, and see their home. I had breakfast and showered, and then I was ready to explore this beautiful city for a couple of days, before we would take our next flight onto the island of Cebu, where her parents lived.

The City of Manila is massive, with many tall buildings and skyscrapers. Even our hotel was very tall. It has great views looking out over the city. So that was it. We spent two wonderful days exploring the city, and I loved the place, the people, and all the different foods I found spicy, and truly delicious.

On our final night in the city, the hotel was holding a UK British X-factor thing. She was very excited as there were some Philippino people singing there she knew of. I was excited too, but there was one thing on my mind from the first day we met at the airport, and it was that I didn't really fancy her. I knew that we were only going to be friends. She was a beautiful, sweet girl, but she had a high-pitched voice, which drove me crazy.

We had a top night at the hotel and the Xfactor, had some talented singers, but one thing went wrong that night. I got very drunk, and she was sober as she is a Muslim. I got all heated up by the show, with the singing and dancing, and I ended up sleeping with her that night.

When I woke up in the morning, I couldn't believe what I had done, as I knew she liked me very much, and I didn't want her to get the wrong idea about us. But I didn't want to upset her either, as I was enjoying her company.

I wanted to experience staying with her family, so I said nothing to her, and she woke next to me, saying, 'Morning, my king,' and she proceeded again to go and get breakfast and bring it to me in bed. We had breakfast together, then she packed our bags, ready to go to the airport for our trip to Cebu to stay with her family.

It was an hour and a half flight to Cebu, and all the way there, she was getting very clingy and affectionate to me, after us sleeping together, which obviously is the normal thing people do. I just felt uncomfortable with it all, and it was doing me nut in, but I just went along with it.

Cebu looked an amazing place in the air, as much as on the ground. We took a taxi to her family home, and of course, when we arrived, I wasn't expecting a brick-built house. Their home was made out of wood, with a cast iron frame, and metal shutters for their roof. Her parents were very pleased to see us both.

She had a younger brother and two big pot-bellied black pigs, which are quite similar to our normal household dogs back home. They were making me laugh, running around us grunting, with their little pig tails going around.

The house was a basic Philippino home, but they were happy as far as I could see. It was a three bedroomed shack, with a small outside open kitchen, and their front room was half outside and half inside, with the TV under the shelter. Their shower was separate from the home, like an outside portaloo. It had running hot water, but it was basically a hose just on a clip, which you stood under to wash yourself.

I didn't understand a word that her family were talking about and had no idea what she was telling her parents about us. I wondered if she was telling them we were an item. They welcomed me in very warmly, and they had some traditional Philippino food waiting for us. The taste and aromas were mouth-watering. It was followed with some cold beers, that they had ready for me, as they knew I drank alcohol. It was an enjoyable night, as we sat outside with a homemade fire, and we all spoke, with her translating everything.

That night we slept together in one of the bedrooms, but to avoid repeating what I'd done, I said I was too tired to have sex, and she was fine with that. The next day when we woke up, her parents had prepared breakfast. It was dried fruit, and the mango was especially tasty, washed down with fresh coconut water.

I stayed a few days, but one day after breakfast and after our showers, I said, 'Let's go for a walk,' which she agreed to. We waved to her parents and her little brother and two black pigs, and off we went. While on our walk, I thanked her for letting me stay, and have the experience, and she said

I was welcome. I asked whether she had told her parents about me, and she said that she had told them we had slept together, and were in a relationship, and thinking of getting married. I was like, *what the fuck.*

I just didn't want to say anything to her to upset her, but all I was worried that this was her territory. Her old man had this big knife that he carried around his waist, for cutting down things and preparing food. If I said something and they didn't like what I said, there might be a problem, so I kept quiet, but in the back on my mind, all I wanted was to get the fuck out of there.

Back at the shack later on, her parents were going shopping to the local market, and she wanted a lie down, so that's when I took the opportunity to make my escape.

I did feel sorry for her and her family, but I didn't know how it would end, when I got to tell her I didn't want a relationship.

While she was asleep, I got my bag, and headed to the main road, to flag a taxi down, and leave. In the taxi, I sent her a message, just saying sorry, and that I didn't set out to hurt anyone, but I didn't want a relationship. I kept it short and sweet, and that was that. I deleted myself off the chatroom, where we had first met.

I was on the move again, by myself, and I felt such a relief. I ended up staying in Cebu for a few more days, in a couple of different hotels, which were amazing. There was one place where the hotel was made with bamboo shoots. To get to the hotel restaurant, which was on a little island by itself, you had to take the hotel boat. It was first class and there was a giant jacuzzi for 25 people or more. One day I was in it with a load of Chinese people and Philippinos, and they asked me if I was the new James Bond star. It was so funny and made me feel mint! Ha ha!

I left Cebo and headed back to Manila, where I stayed back at the Dusit Hotel. One afternoon, I was drinking at one of the hotel bars, and met this man about the same age as me.

He was from Belgium and spoke very good English, and we exchanged stories.

I told him that when I was younger, I used to go to Belgium for the baccy runs, getting rolling tobacco from Ostend, and I had a couple of piss-up weekends in Bruge.

We were both laughing and getting on, and we spoke quite openly, even though the Philippines at that point in time had a massive drug problem, similar to much of the world. The President had waged a war against drugs, for anyone selling them, or taking them, and had them executed on the street by some sort of rebel gang. It's all very political and dangerous to even talk about it.

We sat at the bar for a while, with ice cold San Miguel beers, and then I found out something about the beer. I always thought it was made in Spain. I discovered it's actually brought in from the Philippines, so I learnt something there.

Anyway, we both decided to head out to the city to find some girls and carry on our drinking session. We got a taxi at the front of the hotel, and the Belgian friend said he'd take me to some good bars in the city where girls are. The taxi driver spoke English, and said he knew the right places to take us, so we headed off. He ended up taking us to girl bars, where the girls were for sale, like prostitution. From what I could see they were all quite young and off their heads on drugs. I told the driver and my new friend, it was not for me, so the driver said he knew another place. When we arrived, it was cleaner and more upmarket, but still similar to the first place, and I just wanted to go back to the hotel.

So, I headed back alone. I decided to visit a shopping precinct which was just across the road from the hotel. The place was massive, and I found an Armani exchange shop, and ended up buying a white blazer top. It looked mint, so I wore it straight away, as I had nice jeans on.

I headed to the food court, and after I finished my food, I noticed some girls looking at me. One of them was

Philippino and the other was possibly Japanese. I went over to talk to with them, as they were both beautiful. The Philippino one spoke good English, and we all hit it right off, and they decided to come back with me to the hotel for a drink. At the hotel bar, we were having a really good time, and all of us were flirting with one another. I asked them If they would like to stay for dinner at the hotel and they said yes, which I was very happy about.

I had a lovely time with them, and wanted to treat them, and I wondered which one of them I was going to pull that night. I let them order the food, as I wanted to try different dishes, and I knew they would order things I wasn't familiar with. I'm glad I did as I really enjoyed it.

We finished our food, and I asked them if they would like to join me in my hotel room, for a drink, as I was pretty sure that they were not ready to go home just yet. To my delight, they both said yes, so off we went, and oooh my God, what a night!

They both ended up staying and we all slept with one another, as they were both as horny as fuck and super sexy. What made it especially nice, was that this was my first Japanese lady ever. She even had a full Japanese back tattoo of a dragon, going across the whole of her body. They were both truly so beautiful, and what a top way to finish my stay in the Philippines. It was totally magical, the experience I had there.

CHAPTER TWENTY-ONE

Back on the Costa del Crime, I decided to meet up with one of my mates for a drink down in Fuengirola, to tell him about my holiday. He had a few stories of his own.

One of them was about a person we both knew well. This person lived out in the campo, which means a little off grid out of town, and in the sticks in other words. This man and his wife woke up as normal on just another normal sunny day on the Costa del Sol to a real bad surprise. Three masked men entered the back door of their finca, which is the term for a campo house.

They grabbed hold of him and his wife, and kept asking where all the money, and jewellery were. The couple didn't know what they were talking about, and things were getting very tense. The three men turned the place upside down, looking for cash and valuables. To their shock and surprise, they found nothing, just a few hundred euros.

One of the masked men told the woman to go to the bank, to get their savings out. He warned her that if she told the police, her husband would be a dead man. The lady went off and she didn't tell anyone or call the police. She was worried about her husband. She had to go to three banks to get their life savings out, which was 18,000 euros.

She rang the masked men to say that she had got 18,000 euros, but the men were having none of it. They were screaming down the phone at her to get more, but there was no more.

They became extremely violent, and one of the men put the husband's hand on the table and chopped off two of his fingers, and yet again screamed at her to get more money, before putting the phone down. She phoned them back and told them that she had taken out everything they had, and there was no more.

They said that she should listen on the phone to her husband, as he was screaming in pain, and they then decided to chop two more fingers off. She heard more screams, and they put the phone down on her, after yelling that they wanted more. She couldn't get more, so she headed back to the finca. When she got there, she couldn't believe what she saw, and what they had done to her husband.

Anyway, the three masked men took the 18,000 euros, and did a runner. The poor fuckers, I thought. What a dangerous place this can be. It turned out the intruders had gone to the wrong place. People believe it was supposed to be two fincas up where this wealthy couple lived – crazy!

I also heard too that the porn star that I was talking about earlier, had her villa targeted, and she was in the villa at the time. This time the robbers used sleeping gas through the aircon vents, to knock everyone out. The robbers even took their rings off their hands. Talk about fucking spooky – awful!!

The mate that I was chatting to is a proper funny guy, and into all sorts. He's Dutch and in his mid-twenties. He was telling me this story of moving some money about. On the day he instructed his driver to drop off 23,000 euros to another driver at McDonalds near the waterpark at Fuengirola, and it had to be bang on time at 5pm, and it would be a black Golf GTi for the money to be passed to.

Anyway, his driver got there on the dot, and saw a black GTi in the carpark. He pulled alongside the vehicle, and the other driver was in the car, with music on and the windows down, and they both nodded to each other. As instructed, the driver placed the small sports bag with the money in it into the GTi, and just drove off. Then my mate had a call off the other people, indicating that they were running late, and would be there for 5.15pm. He told them that his driver had just called him, to confirm he'd made the drop already.

Well, you could imagine, now there's this bloke with 23,000 euros, that has just been given it for fuck all! My mate said, he instructed his driver to get back there dead sharpish, as there had been a mistake. His driver went back there a few minutes later and couldn't believe his luck, as the black GTi was still there. The man at the wheel was looking confused and scared, having looked in the bag and seen the money.

The driver pulled up beside him, apologised, and said, 'Look, say no more.' He gave him 100 euros, took the bag back, and while he was doing this, the real black Golf GTi turned up. I just couldn't stop laughing, at how lucky they were. Most people would have seen that money and bolted and thought happy days.

Time for me on the Costa del Sol was going great, and with my health too, as my chest and bones weren't as bad as in the cold and rainy weather back in Blighty. It really is surprising what hot and sunny weather can do for your health.

It was a good year too, as I had just started setting up a marble polishing company, with my pal who was in his fifties, and loved a pint or two. He was from County Durham near Newcastle, and his whole family were lovely. We all became very close, and we were doing places like villas, apartments and shops, and we even had a contract at a hotel called Las Palmeras taking pigeon shit off the roof, polishing their ground floors, and their outside apartment terraces. It was a hot, sticky and dangerous job in the heat and sun, as pigeon shit can be absorbed into your skin, and make you very ill. We had to wear suitable clothing and masks.

I had my hands into everything really, with having a few cars out to rent too, and on this particular year, I went back and forth out of Morocco, as I had met a beautiful girl there. I had made a few Moroccan mates, who were related to one of the top Moroccan cartel families. I spent many more amazing nights at the top Tangier hotel, the El Minzar. I met the head Chief of the Tangier police department at the bar, and we hit it off after having a few drinks, and to be honest he was a bent as a two-pound note.

On this particular holiday, my best mate Norm was with me, and it was his first time in Morocco, but he didn't really like the place. He decided to go back to Spain so I headed off on a trip with my girlfriend and Moroccan friends, to see the Atlas Mountains. It was a crawling fifteen-hour jeep ride, but what an amazing place it is up there. The views are beautiful, and panoramic. This can also be a dangerous place as it's used for major drug trafficking routes, with little police or authorities can do. But many are paid off.

I really was enjoying my time in Morocco, especially the cuisine. I adore cous-cous and Moroccan lamb. It's got to be the best lamb, apart from New Zealand, in the world. The only thing I didn't like here, was that the cost of alcoholic drinks was sky high with this being a Muslim country. Anyway, it was another lovely trip, yet again.

Back in Spain, it was coming to the end of a great year, and I had decided to join one of my good mates to a trip to India. Before I left, I headed over to see the kids, before my Xmas trip to India. I had a lovely few days seeing them, and then I was off.

CHAPTER TWENTY-TWO

India here we come!

We were staying in Goa, near Panaji in the Miramu beach resort, and we had a top notch 5-star hotel, all singing all dancing, and right on the beach. The hotel had five different restaurants to cater for different tastes. It really was a mint place.

Panaji was crazy, with all its traffic and hustle and bustle of lots of people moving about, and all the different shops selling their foods, and tea bars and restaurants. I came across a proper Lacoste shop, and it was all dirt cheap compared to back home in Blighty, or Spain. So, I ended up buying loads of things.

One day we headed out on a trip to see the mountains inland, where they make the tea, and we ended up at the beautiful massive waterfall where we could take a dip and cool off from the Indian heat. It was amazing, with loads of little monkeys running around and nicking people's clothing as they took a dip, which I thought was hilarious.

Back on the coastline, we explored many beaches and places, with one of my favourite beaches called Baga beach. We stopped at one of our mate's bars. They were a Dutch couple who had been living there for years and had really made it their home. We spent that day there with a four-course meal, two bottles of wine, and brandy for after. The whole lot came to thirty pounds, cheap as chips. Each night we would end up in some of the nightclubs, and I tell you what, some places really did kick.

Then there was the night of all nights. Yes, the Full Moon Party! This was in a totally opposite place to Thailand's on the beaches. This time it was held in a dense woodland area, and yet again, thousands of weird and strange people were there, with everybody off their trollies, with all types of music.

I met a guy from Germany. He had been living in India for many years. He was a proper old school hippy. He told me he no longer holds a passport, doesn't have a mobile phone, or any electrical items, and lives off grid, and off the land. He had made a wooden tree house, which he lived in, and he was a vegetarian, living off lentils and rice.

I asked him how he managed for money, and he said he makes little bead necklaces and bracelets. I ended up buying one and was quite fond of it anyway. He was quite an interesting man, but was on another planet. He was off his nut on mushrooms, and with smoking this really smelly skunk weed. To be honest, he reminded me of an Ewok, those hairy little creatures that live in treehouses in those Star Wars movies. He was ever so funny. Well, this night was a totally mad and a truly amazing night. The whole place was just kicking and totally off the wall, and it took me the whole of the next day back at the hotel to recover.

In one of the hotel's many bars, I met a guy called Nassem or something. He was a very smart, young Indian man and we all got talking as he kept coming in and out of the bar and was treated like royalty by the hotel staff. He told us he lived next door to the hotel, and could see from the beach this place was like a massive Indian palace. He said he was the prince of Goa. Whether he was or not I never found out, but I knew he was proper loaded. People did treat him like a prince, and he was a very smart and educated guy.

We planned to meet up on Xmas day at the hotel for the Xmas day food and the evening party. It was a great night, a proper toast to the festive season, and it finished in the early hours of the morning when we all decided to go back to his palace, with all of us getting in on it.

It was 6am in the morning. I was completely exhausted with it being such a top night. I left the palace, tip toeing past all these Indian housekeepers, asleep on the hard floor on thin mats.

Back in the hotel, the atmosphere was totally different to the former festive atmosphere. Everyone was looking at the hotel TVs and some were in shock and crying. It was terrible. I headed back to my room to shower, and get into bed. I turned my TV on to see what all the fuss was about and I just couldn't believe what I was seeing. A massive tsunami had struck Asia, killing thousands of people with lots missing. With its destruction it had wiped out the coastlines, hotels, restaurants and whole villages. The worst place being hit was Phuket in Thailand. It was total devastation, and very upsetting to watch.

I woke up later on in the afternoon and was so shattered after the party. I rushed to the hotel pool to find my mate, as he had left the party much earlier than me. We began talking about the tsunami. He turned to me and said that we were very lucky really, as a Phuket resort was where we were going to go first, but he changed his mind at the last minute.

As we were on the subject of Thailand, we both started talking about another time when I was there. It was New Year's Eve and on that particular night, it was almost midnight and I had been drinking all day long, and I was totally pissed and in high spirits. I decided to go shopping to kill some time before my flight back to Spain. I ended up in the sunglasses shop and was trying on a lovely pair of gold Armani ones. With me being so pissed, I put them on top of my head and looked at some more, totally forgetting that I was still wearing them on my head, and I left the shop without realising.

About an hour late with not long before my flight due to depart, the shop manager and the police found me wandering around on the security cams. They put me in handcuffs and nicked me, and took me back to the sunglasses shop, with a policeman recording the whole incident. I swore that I didn't know they were there, with me being so pissed. Anyway, they were having none of it, but the shop manager said, 'You pay for them and you have no problem,' but I had very little cash on me, so we tried my two bank cards, to pay for the glasses, but I had been in Thailand for a month, and I had fuck all left to give. I'm thinking shit, I need help, what a nightmare this is, with my flight about to depart very soon.

The situation couldn't have been any worse. The manager kept saying to me that I needed to pay, or I would go to prison, and in Thailand, stealing is a very bad offence, which could get you years instead of months, like back home, and I was shitting myself. The police told me that I had thirty minutes to pay, so I'd better think of something or I was going to have to go with them, end of. They let me use the phone to call a couple of people, but with it being New Year's Eve, and the time difference, nobody answered. So, my hopes there came to an end. The only thing I could think of was to ask the public if they could help, as they could see the situation I was in, cuffed and being held by the police. I needed to find English speaking people.

Finally, this English bloke stopped and listened to what had happened, and God bless him, he didn't have much cash, but this kind man gave me all he had left from his holiday, but explained he was skint too, with no money left on his cards either, but I thanked him. Unfortunately, it wasn't enough, but I was making headway. I tried and tried again with people and the time was ticking, with my thirty minutes now up, with me thinking welcome to the Bangkok Hilton, that I knew about from books and TV.

Then, to my surprise, this American lady, stopped and asked what was going on. I explained it all and told her that I would be going to prison if I didn't pay the money. She called me a silly man, but she said she would help, in the spirit of New Year, as she didn't want me to go to prison. To my relief, she said she would pay the whole lot off. I just couldn't believe my luck.

CHAPTER TWENTY-THREE

Getting over my jetlag back in Spain after my trip to India, things were good, but for my poor mum back in the UK, things were getting worse, although I was unaware of it as she didn't want to worry me.

I had met this English girl on an online dating site. We met close to Hemel Hempstead, when I was going back and forth to see my kids, and we became very close with us falling in love. She moved across to Spain with me, and her two kids, which was a bit of a sore subject, to my own two kids.

They thought they had lost their dad, because of her two kids, which was never the case. My two were still young and didn't understand that sometimes things change when you are in a relationship with somebody. It caused my own daughter not to come over on holiday, which was very sad to me, but I always made sure I went over to see her. My daughter is everything to me.

About a year and a half had passed with me and my girlfriend still together. I noticed as I was flying back and forth to see my kids, Mum was frailer, and her breathing was terrible. I was ever so worried when she told me she was getting home help from a nurse coming and going, and checking up on her, but that she was fine with my stepdad around to help her. She said I was not to worry, but in the back of my mind I continued to worry.

In Spain, I would ring all the time, to remain in contact with her. As time went on her voice was becoming even more breathless, as she chatted to me over the phone, which was making me uncomfortable with worry. Then, there was this one night, me and my girlfriend decided to have a little party. We had one every now and then. A few bottles of wine, with a little bit of coke, and I put my phone on silent, as sometimes people just ring to ask about hire cars at all hours of the night. We had a good night, and must have crashed out in the early hours, with us both waking up around 11am the next morning.

To my surprise when I looked at my phone, there was a missed call from my mum at around 4am UK time, with it being 5am in Spain. Straight away I called her back, but there was no answer, so I just thought she had gone back to bed to sleep, bless her. I decided to ring back later, or she would return the call when she woke up and saw a missed call from me.

About an hour later the phone rang, and I rushed to answer it, when I saw it was my mum on the caller ID. But on answering, it was my stepdad, and I thought to myself, how strange. Anyway, he said, 'Lloyd, I'm sorry, son, but I've got some really bad news.'

My heart raced, as I knew something bad was up, as my stepdad never has my mum's phone.

Then he said, 'Son.' There was a pause.

I started to sweat, and I thought I had swallowed my tongue. Then he told me my mum had died. As we both burst into tears, my whole body was shaking, and I collapsed. I was a complete mess at first, telling him down the phone that she hadn't died, and he replied, 'Son, she has.' My whole world collapsed around me, and with a stabbing feeling in my heart, I asked him how she had died.

He told me that she had died in the early hours of the morning, and the ambulance had come, and there would be an inquest. To my shock, I remembered the missed phone call, and I said, 'Dad, did you ring me at 4am?'

He replied, 'No son.'

I said, 'Well Mum did then.' I had missed the call from her. She probably knew it was her time, and was calling me to say a final goodbye, which led me to break down even more, as I wasn't there for her to say goodbye. My girlfriend had to grab hold of me, as I was collapsing onto the hard marble floor. I just knew from this day my life would never feel the same again.

Days went past and I was a complete mess, and drinking heavily. I started to smoke cigarettes and snort loads of Cocaine. I was out of control. My girlfriend did her best to comfort me. Two weeks later I was flying over for the funeral which was at Watford, where we said our farewells at the local Swan pub where I used to drink. A good few hundred people saw her off, which was really nice, as my family was well known.

On my return back to Spain, my girlfriend said that we should get married, and I said yes straight away, as I thought I would make my mum proud, by finally settling down. We had been with each other for around two years. I was thinking that my mum who was my rock had passed away, and my girlfriend is now my future rock. We booked our wedding in Gibraltar with the Botanica Gardens for our reception, and we spent our honeymoon at the famous Rock Hotel, with the best suite they had.

Even on our wedding day, I was off my nut, snorting lines of pure Cocaine rock on the Rock of Gibraltar. It really was a good wedding, and honeymoon, but I wasn't right in the head. I thought at the time this was the best thing to do, after my mum passing. As time went past in our married life, we enjoyed holidays, and love with each other, and these were some really good times, but with my drug abuse and heavy drinking it took a toll on us both.

Out of the blue, another disaster struck us. Her brother was killed in a fatal car crash, which affected my wife in a really bad way, bless her. So now, we were both grieving. Me with my mum and her with her brother. So, we were both going through very hard times, which led us into heavy drinking and other things. All my work that I was meant to be doing wasn't getting done, and we both weren't getting out of bed. We were losing the plot.

My wife left me to go to the UK for the funeral, and I stayed and looked after the kids, but she overstayed, and left me for a month. I wasn't coping too well, but nor was she. She had fallen into the same explosive life of heavy drinking and drug taking, with this causing a massive impact on our lives and finances.

We had a lot of arguments, and on top of this, the girlfriend of her brother that had passed away, had just given birth and was having problems looking after the baby. My wife wanted to take the baby on, but I was in no fit state at all for this, so I said no, which made us have even more arguments, with her deciding to move back to the UK with the kids.

I ended up staying alone in Spain, and I'm afraid this was the end of our marriage. I didn't want to come back to the UK, and leave my mum, as I had put her ashes on the top of Mijas Mountain. It wasn't a messy divorce, and it was a shame really, as she was a top lady, with me holding some good memories. I wished her all the best for the future when I heard she had remarried.

It took me a long time to pull myself out of my dark hole, but I had to as I was killing myself. Also, with my finances, I was behind on my mortgage and many more bills. So, I sold my cars except one for one that I drove, I paid all my bills off and started to get my life back on track.

I went to Gibraltar for a hire car company, and that is where I started something new out in Gibraltar. Yes, the tobacco runs! In doing them, I met some of the biggest players in the game! I even did a few little walk throughs myself in and out of the border, stashing the tobacco anywhere; down my pants, in my socks, you name it I did it.

On the Spanish side of the border, you had the Guardia police enforcing it, with this one police lady enforcing it with an iron fist. Her nickname was Super Bitch. Once she had her eye on you, she just wouldn't give up. But of course, being Spain, you still had many corrupt ones on the border who were getting paid a lot for turning a blind eye.

There was this one time I went down there for the whole day and I got myself up to fifty cartons, walking in and out a few times with friends. Then, just as I was pulling off in my car, an undercover copper who had been watching us all day came over and nicked me. So, I lost the lot, and got a big fine, but that's how it is down there.

Another time, I had over one hundred cartons, and got stopped on the way back to Fuengirola by the police rolling roadblock, and yet again lost the lot, and got a massive fine this time. So, we were up and down in this, but believe you me, I had some good days.

I was a bit down on my luck after that roadblock, and I certainly didn't see this one coming, but I had a bit of luck coming my way at last. I only went and won the Euromillions Lottery!

It wasn't a life changing amount, I'm telling you it was a fair few quid, talk about Jackpot. It was at a time when I needed it. The lift it gave me was amazing, and the bloke behind the counter started to shake, when he scanned my ticket. To be honest I was gutted, as I was one number out of winning proper money, millions, but I was still happy and excited with what I got.

I treated myself to a Malaga season ticket and had many great days and nights up at the stadium, with my Spanish hairdresser Antonio. A load of us used to go there, but I was the only Englishman in this mob. I even took my son to the games, the big ones they play like Madrid and Barcelona. We saw them all. It was pure magic! I was absolutely smashing it in all directions. The hire cars, marble flooring and other avenues were buzzing with life.

On top of all this, my daughter gave birth to my first granddaughter. I was over the moon with delight, and what a marvellous beautiful girl she is! I was so proud of them both, and me being a young grandfather at the age of 34 years old. There was new light and new life to my family, and my mother above would be so happy in seeing this. I flew them both over often and rented them nice apartments and put them up in nice hotels. We were all loving it.

I remember one time coming to see them for Xmas and taking them for an amazing Xmas dinner in St Albans at Jamie Oliver's restaurant. After dinner I went in the bookies while they waited outside, and I put a lump on the dogs, trap 1, and it rocketed home and only won! So, we had a split on that, which was great!

CHAPTER TWENTY-FOUR

Back in Spain I met this new beautiful lady through a friend of mine. She was a real stunner, who was an ex- Miss Spain, and she had won her region and became Miss Barcelona, but the only trouble with it was, she was up her own arse, which did my nut in. So, after a while, I dumped her, and she turned around and said, 'You can't do that! I'm Miss...'

Before she could say anything else, I told her, 'And I'm Lloyd of the Dance,' and I danced her right off, and that was the end of that!

I was still having my moments, getting on it, but very rarely, as I was always pining and missing my mum, but I had to control myself. What good would I be dead, to my lovely girls and son?

Then, I met this beautiful girl down in Marbella in Puerto Banus. She was half Colombian, and half Panamanian, as her mother was Colombian and her father was from Panama. And wow, she was out of the box! I mean, I have had my fair share of sexy ladies, but this was the tops. I met her through her cousin who I was good close friends with, who lived up past Malaga, in a place called Velez Malaga.

We met at the Malaga Football Stadium, on match nights. Me and this new girl hit it right off and she started to stay at mine when she was in Spain, with me also flying in and out of South America to see her.

I loved doing this, as South America is one of my favourite places on the planet, where there is so much for me to explore. I stayed many times in the City of Panama hotels, and in our flat, and it was great over there. I did the Panama Canal, went sea fishing, and I also went exploring a little of the dangerous Darien Gap. This is a jungle in Panama, which adjoins Colombia. This area is great for wildlife, but is also a notorious drug route, for the

Colombians to traffic their product, Cocaine. It goes into Panama, then through central South America, then into Mexico, and up to the USA, where they get more money for the Cocaine, or it's shipped out to Europe.

Back in Spain, a friend came to visit me, and he asked me if I knew anyone that I could put him onto as he had a job he needed doing. I had a quick think about it. Then I said yes. I said I wanted nothing to do with it, but I would introduce him to some boys I knew from Hull. Time went on and they were working together, but I didn't know the ins and outs as I said from the start of it all.

Then, I had a phone call from the boys in Hull, asking if I minded picking some money up from the London side, as they knew I was going over to the UK to see my kids at the time. I thought it was harmless, so it would be okay. It was only money and they were giving me a big drink for doing it. So, I thought, oh well, that will pay for my whole trip, plus a little more for after collecting the money from the London side, running it up to them in Hull.

So, that was it, I landed at Heathrow Airport, and within an hour I was with the London contact, but without my knowledge or his, the NCA were watching us, (National Crime Agency). I had returned to Spain when two months later I heard from a mutual friend of the London side, that they were all getting nicked. I thought fuck that, that's why I have little to do with that work, if at all.

Then two weeks later the bomb came. I had another phone call with them saying that the police at the NCA were interested in me. At first, I laughed, and thought what the fuck for, I've done nothing wrong. But then it set in and I was like OMG for fucks sake! Then I calmed myself down, thinking okay, if they are interested in me, they will work it all out, and see that I have fuck all to do with it, apart from picking up the money.

So, for the next week or so I just waited to hear anything more, and I was in good spirits about it, as I knew I hadn't really done anything, only picked some money up, and had a conversation. Then I got another call from the same person who said that my name was defo on the NCA paperwork. He said that both he and I knew I wasn't a big part of it, so they would probably work that out. Our conversation ended with him telling me that I probably had nothing to worry about.

Then, I was thinking, what the hell have I got myself involved in? My head was working overtime with worry, and I decided to take his advice. Lie low and keep out of the way, while all the mess is sorted out with them seeing I was a minor part of it, and then my life could return to normal again. So, I packed my car up, and decided to just get away from it all.

Yes, I was sort of running away. I felt terrible, so low. I took my little Doberman Pinscher with me, but I left my French Bulldog behind, as he was suffering with epilepsy, bless him, and it would be too much for him, moving all around the place. I left him with a dear friend who had a big villa, where I knew he would be fine and well looked after, and I knew one day I would go and collect him, but I was ever so sad saying goodbye.

The next big thing was I had a chat with my mum up on the mountain where I had laid her ashes, telling her the mess I had got myself into, and that I was sorry to let her down, first with that missed phone call, and now all the shit I was in.

I was ever so tearful as I pulled away in my car, looking in the rear-view mirror as I was heading off, saying my goodbyes, and wondering when the next time would be when I would get to spend time with her. I was a complete mess and even my girlfriend had split with me because of this.

So, that was it. I left my old life behind for now, and was hoping to return once all this mess had blown over. I headed up to Alicante to stay with a friend I had known for years. I settled in quite easily as I'm the kind of person who makes friends quickly, and I could live anywhere in the world.

With things being on the up, I had heard no more about the case going on back home in the UK. This made me think they'd worked it all out, and realised I wasn't a big part of it. I started to feel a little happy again, as a year and a half went by with no problems.

Then the big bomb comes straight out of the blue. Shit was about to really hit the fan!

CHAPTER TWENTY-FIVE

I was arrested in early September. I remember this very well, as two of my best pals had just flown over from London. One of my pals had three sons who lived in Alicante, and he was visiting them at the same time, so we all decided to meet.

I knew a quiet little area with beautiful beach, bars and nice restaurants, so I suggested a nice Chinese place for us to eat at, as they had a Menu de Die, which means menu of the day, which I thought was great value for a large family. There were five courses for seven euros, including a bottle of wine.

It was nice to see them all, and we spent ages chatting and laughing. They were all aware that I'd moved to the area because of all the bad that had happened to me in Malaga, and they were commenting that I looked as though I was doing well for myself. I was always in the car hire business, but there I tried something new and established a rent-a-bicycle scheme, which was starting to change for the better.

After the meal finished, my friends dropped their cars and their nan back to the hotel, then met me back at my place. When they came back, we had a few beers and some Cocaine. We had a great time with lots of music and chatting. After a while they had to go to their families at the hotel. When they left, I was still buzzing, so I rang my girlfriend and asked her to come over. She got a taxi as she couldn't drive, and shortly after she arrived, we were partying with music on the stereo and porn on the TV.

We woke up at midday on Sunday, and it was very hot outside. The aircon was on, but as we had been fucking during the night, and we were shattered. I didn't want to do much other than take my dog out for a walk, and then spend the day chilling at home to recover. My girlfriend was going to meet a friend in the city, so she got ready, then we had a light lunch, kissed each other goodbye, and she left on the bus. I couldn't wait to see her again.

It was Monday. I woke up first thing, had a brew, fed my dog and then my Moroccan girlfriend and I were sending naughty Whatsapp messages to one another, and then I returned to bed with my brew and to relieve myself, ha ha. That was it, I was ready for the day, so I chucked on clothes and took the dog for a walk.

It was around 10am and the day was already heating up, so we went for a picturesque walk, with the mountains on one side and the Mediterranean on the other. We were walking inland up a little lane with no traffic whatsoever, only beautiful fields of oranges growing. I decided to take a bag full, so that I could make the very best squeezed orange juice that it's possible to make.

I was still tired from the other night and was still sweating the booze out of my system, and so I decided to head for home for a nice cold shower. I got back, stuck my electric bike on charge. I went everywhere on that electric bike, as I don't like to drink and drive, and usually when I'm out, I'll end up on a beachfront, either with friends, or people I've never met before, and I'll have a couple of cheeky beers. I love talking to anybody, which is a trait straight from my mum, as she was just the same.

Then I jumped in the shower with MTV tunes pumping out. After the shower, I got ready. I had my shades on, my shorts and flip flops on, and my man bag containing my phone and a bit of change. I knew I wouldn't need much cash, as I was meeting a friend who owed me a few drinks.

I put the radio on for the dog and locked the door. I didn't know it was going to be one of the worst days of my life. I also didn't know that there was a European arrest warrant out for me. I thought it was just going to be another normal day – NOT!!

I was walking down a hill with my arm on my bike. I wanted to stop for an ice cream as it was so hot. I noticed a man walking towards me, and instantly I recognised him as a tramp, who was sitting on some steps begging a few days earlier. I was about to stop to give him a euro for some food or drink, but as I approached him, he stopped me. I didn't think anything of his actions, as I just thought he was desperate for a drink.

He said, 'Amigo – To nombre Senor Wright?' This means is your name Mr Wright? I was like, what the fuck? 'Yes, who are you?'

Before I knew what was happening, he pulled out his gun and police badge, and told me I was under arrest. Within seconds there were lots of armed police surrounding me. There were some in cars, some on foot and even one on a pushbike. It was like something out of a movie. The whole street stopped to watch, and people seemed afraid and shocked, as the police were wearing normal clothing and it was only when the uniformed officers appeared, that people relaxed a little, as they knew it wasn't a shootout between villains.

One officer who was in front of me asked, 'Where's your gun?' and I replied, 'Who the hell is telling you that I'm a person like that?'

I was sweating like anything and scared and shocked, and my heart was pumping in my chest like I was going to have a heart attack. It wasn't helped by the fact that he'd put the handcuffs on too tight. There were now loads of police and enough armour on show to shoot out an Afghan terrorist group. I thought it was a bit much, and wondered who the hell did they think I was.

I asked what it was all about, but the officer just said we were going to the main station in Alicante to discuss it there. Just then, I saw a friend witnessing what was happening, and I asked the police if I could give him my bike and house keys so he could go and let the dog out, and surprisingly enough they agreed. I was relieved for my poor old dog.

Then all I could think of was what I'd just been through. Up until that point, it had been so hard changing and leaving my old life behind, and making a fresh start, and now this had happened. I was a mess, weak, stressed and I felt like my heart was about to give up on me. I thought enough was enough. Would I be able to make it through this living nightmare? Was I strong enough for the road ahead, and what would happen to me next?

There were three policemen in the car that drove me to the city, all armed to the teeth. They were mostly young men really and were covered in tattoos. If it wasn't for the police badges, I would have thought I was being kidnapped by a load of steroid laden football thugs.

They were laughing at me a lot. I lied to them and told them I didn't speak much Spanish, but all the while I was listening to them. They were saying things like, look at him with all of his tattoos, and they were checking out my watch and then talking about my flip flops and man bag. They kept looking me up and down, and I thought to myself, you a bunch of faggots, keep your eyes to yourselves.

It took around an hours' drive to arrive at the station. I was starting to dehydrate. I needed water, and my heart was still the same. My mind was going crazy. I was in a bad way, and just wanted to get out of the car, especially with these poofs eyeing me up

It was now 2pm and we had arrived at the city police station. An electric garage opened, and we drove in. I hadn't realised there were two more police cars following us – talk about an armed convoy! I got out of the car still handcuffed. There were police everywhere, and a man with a camcorder, and press taking photos of me. I thought to myself, who do they think I am, Pablo Escobar? But this was no joke, it was really happening to me.

They took me into a room where they had an interpreter, who made sure I fully understood what was happening. I was thinking it must be linked to my friend who got arrested in the UK.

The interpreter said, 'Mr Wright, we have no problem with you here in Spain, but in the UK, you face some serious charges.'

At first, I thought what you mean serious? But I didn't speak. Then I thought, serious is picking up a lot of money. Is this all about that? Then, the interpreter said, 'The charges are very serious. You are up for one count of conspiracy to supply class A drugs, Cocaine and one charge of supplying class B drugs cannabis.'

I was like, 'NO, NO, NO, this isn't true. Oh my God, I can't believe this is all happening to me.' I felt so sick and I felt my heart race so much at one point I thought it might just give up on me. I asked, 'What happens to me now?'

He explained that I could fight the extradition at court, but because the accusations were so serious, I would lose. He then said that if I chose to fight it, the process would take longer, and cost a lot of money which they wouldn't be happy about, but in the end, I would end up back in the UK.

I told them straight away that I wouldn't fight it, as I wanted to go back to the UK. I wanted to go back and clear my name.

He stood up and said, 'That's good Mr Wright,' then he walked out of the room, and I said, 'Thank you and goodbye.'

The three policemen wanted to talk to me constantly, photograph me, take my fingerprints, and finally they said they wanted to strip search me. I bet they do, I thought, bloody poofs.

After that they asked if I had any drugs or money, and even the gun that they'd mentioned earlier at the arrest. They asked if there was anything back at the apartment, where I'd left my dog. I replied, 'No, for fucks sake, I don't have any of these things back at the apartment. I'm not that sort of person. The information you've been given is wrong, and whoever has given you it must be taking crack.'

I couldn't believe all of this was happening to me, and I knew I was in deep trouble. Then I had a thought that if I was hiding any of those things back at the apartment, the police had let me give my keys to my friend to go and get my dog. Any friend would surely remember to remove incriminating items like that, if I'd had them at the apartment. It made me think how unprofessional the police had been though, by letting me give him the keys.

Then, they told me it was time to be locked up in one of their lovely cells. They explained that they would bring some food, and then they would come for me at 5am to travel to Madrid. I thought, shit, I'm so tired and stressed and worried. I needed to eat, and I thought they were taking the piss by getting me up at 5am. I realised that I only had 3 euros in my man bag, and now I needed money for calls, food and other shit, if they put me in prison awaiting extradition.

But then I thought money was the least of my problems. I lay on my super thin mattress. The food they brought was shit. Eventually, I began to fall asleep, as I was so exhausted. It was around 9pm. What a shit long day it had been. Then, I began to think about how much more shit was ahead of me.

Bang on target at 5am, they arrived. I'd had a shit night, and the police were at my cell door already. I thought to myself, bloody hell, in the whole 15 years that I'd lived in Spain, not once were the Spanish on time. Normally they're late, or it's manana, manana, which usually means tomorrow. Wakey, wakey hands on my snakey!! But for some reason I didn't have a stiffy, so I knew it was going to be another grim day ahead. It was a shame my girlfriend wasn't with me, otherwise I would have said, 'Brew for a screw.' I didn't want to say that to the three policemen from yesterday, who were now standing at my door, although they would probably have enjoyed that, the bloody poofs.

So, that was it, I was up and ready. They gave me a quick coffee but didn't offer me a screw as well. Then, they told me that I didn't have time for a shower. I thought we must be in a rush to the airport for a quick flight to Madrid, so I enquired, 'J Aeroporto? And to my surprise they replied,

'No amigo, couche,' which means that we were travelling by car. I thought shit, it's about six hours drive.

I was pissed off, and my whole body was still aching from the mattress. My arms and wrists were sore from the handcuffs. I hadn't slept much at all, and I was a bit smelly as I'd had to go without a shower. I was drained mentally, and now really pissed off. I felt like crying deep down, but just to myself.

I was handcuffed again and put in the normal police car with the same three officers, who were still armed to the teeth. In a second car were more police and more guns like a mini armoured convoy, to protect the whole of the USA going to Madrid for diplomatic talks.

As the electric doors of the garage opened, the convoy spun out, with lights and sirens blazing. I thought OMG, here we go again, it's a bit much isn't it? We raced through the city, sliding in and out of the traffic, with some crazy driving, jumping through red lights, and not stopping at roundabouts, driving straight into the traffic with lights flashing. It was awful in the back of the car as the seats were a hard plastic, which meant my arse was sliding all over the place. At the same time my arse was already going numb and we'd only just got out of the city.

As we left the city, I saw the signs for Madrid on the Carretta (motorway) – 550 kilometers. I took one look at it and knew it was going to be a long time sitting on this piece of plastic chair. My body was already in pain, my back, legs and arse, as well as my arms and hands, as yet again I was in handcuffs which were too tight. I did mention it to them, but they just laughed, the mugs. I tried to compose myself and think good thoughts, but it was hard as the pain was torture.

We were now zooming down the motorway. The sirens had been turned off, but the lights were still on to warn the other drivers to move out of the way, as we were coming up their arse very quickly. Luckily, the aircon was on in the car, which was the only comfort as the temperature outside was already very hot. This one thing helped me out so much.

Without it I think I would have passed out from this torture.!!

I was falling in and out of sleep, the type where your head tilts as you drop off and then all of a sudden, you're awake again – horrible. I glimpsed out of the window in desperation to look for a motorway sign, to see how far we had got on this mentally draining journey. I spotted one and we were about halfway with 256 km to go. I was so weak, and my heart problem was kicking in again, and I needed water. 'Por favor, mi queiro, aqua.' (Please water, I want water) I said and then I told them I was in pain.

After 20km or so we pulled over for refreshments, and in my mind, we were at an oasis in the desert, and was about to get a nice cold beer, and a slice of pizza, with a bar of chocolate for dessert. To my surprise, the officer came back with the smallest bottle of water, and that ended my little dream. 'Gracias,' I said, thanking him, but in my mind, I was thinking what a prick.

We were nearly there and were driving so fast that Lewis Hamilton would have raised a smile. I thought, at last, as we approached the main route and went past many clubs. It felt surreal wondering what they would say if I asked them to pull up to one of the fanny clubs, even though there was no chance.

When I looked out of the window, I realised we were going around in circles, then I heard one of them say they couldn't remember the way to the entrance of the European High courts, because of roadworks that were going on. I thought why the fuck is this happening to me? Then, the driver stopped and asked two local policemen for directions.

At last, we approached a huge building and entered through an underground parking area. We all got out of the car, and I was the last one out as I needed assistance due to the handcuffs. When I stood up, I thought my legs were going to give way. They ushered me through some doors to a reception area, where they signed me in and asked if I needed a lawyer. I told them I did. My body was in a bad way as well as my heart, and I felt like I'd done twelve rounds with Mike Tyson. Finally, they took me to a cell where I could wait for them in luxury – NOT!

I pressed the bell in my cell as it smelt so bad, or it was me, or more likely a bit of both. Luckily for me it was a female officer, and she was super fit in her uniform. I thought it would be nice to jump in the shower with her, even if she wanted to cuff me lol.

The officer was nice enough and said I could shower, and provided me with soap and a towel, and it was heaven, like my first ever shower, like I was a shower virgin. My body shook under the water, but it felt so good. I went back to my cell and straight to sleep.

I slept for about two hours until the door was opened at 3pm, and I was informed that a doctor was waiting for me. They took me to him, and he asked if the police had harmed me, and I told him they hadn't. He examined me and told me my heart was quite jumpy, and gave me some tablets to help me, and some cream to apply to my skin where the handcuffs had been, and also some painkillers and a sleeping tablet. I thanked him and was taken back to the cell. I was told it was too late to go to court, so my lawyer would come at 11am the next day. So, this was going to be my first night.

I laid on the bed and thought about all the things I'd experienced in my life. Just when I was beginning to sort out my fucked-up mind, and getting ready to sleep, I heard banging, shouting and fighting. It was going off big time. From what I could hear, the man wasn't Spanish. Then I heard people being thrown all over the place, and groans of pain. Finally, I heard the cell door slam shut, and realised they must have put him in the cell next to me, and it went quiet. I really didn't need this shit. Just a few minutes passed before the person in the cell next door started kicking and banging. I was so stressed and tired, and I thought, welcome to hell.

After about two hours of the madness, the noise was beginning to die down. He must have been tiring out, or I hoped he was. I'd spent the last hour, shouting at him to shut the fuck up, and telling him to fuck off, and loads more shit as well, as I was losing the plot. After about another hour it ended, and that was my sign to try and get to sleep, so that I was ready for my lawyer in the morning. My head was spinning, thinking about it all. Luckily my sleeping pill was kicking in, and my eyes were closing at last.

CHAPTER TWENTY-SIX

I woke very early, even with the sleeping pill, as would anyone with the weight of the world on their shoulders. I'd had a broken night of sleep, but I had slept a bit, and was feeling a lot better than the night before.

It was 7am and for the next three hours I sat in my cell, waiting for the lawyer to come. My head was in a right mess. The lawyer arrived at around 10am and pretty much repeated what the translator had said. I said I didn't want to fight it, I just wanted to get back to the UK to sort it out, and explain it was not true. I did tell the lawyer that I'd picked some money up from somebody and that's all this must be related to.

I sat in the courtroom with the judge talking, and a few people tapping on their laptops. It was like my life was being passed around between them. My lawyer explained that I wanted to go to the UK to sort this mess out, so the judge said that I'd be sent to prison while the UK and Spanish authorities sorted out the paperwork. I asked how long it would take, and he answered that it could be as long as six months. I thought, great that's all I need. I wanted to get back to the UK so I could sort out my life which was now in tatters. I thanked my lawyer even though he didn't have much to do, and he said, 'Good luck Mr Wright, I hope all goes well.'

The police marched me back to my cell, and as we got closer, it was obvious that the man in the next cell had woken up, as I could hear banging and shouting. He was kicking off big time. It sounded like they had King Kong caged in there. Great, I thought. No chance of an afternoon nap (siesta). This is a joke. Is anything going to go right for me?

A couple of hours passed, and the noise next door didn't seem to get any quieter. It was a nightmare. I shouted back a few times, 'Hijo la pute,' (son of a bitch), but he just got louder. After a while my door opened, and a police officer stood there with some food for me. He said that I wasn't going anywhere today, and that I'd leave for prison in the morning. Great, I thought, I'm going to have a lovely night next to this ape King Kong.

Yet again I didn't have a good night's sleep, and the ape didn't either. I just couldn't wait to get the hell out of there and away from the greyback next door. It was about 9am when the door opened, and they said, 'That's it we're taking you to prison (Sato del Real) now.'

'Let's go,' I said, with the relief that I'd be getting away from the madness. Then to my surprise, they opened the ape's door, and I thought, what's going on. He stepped out and I nearly swallowed my tongue and filled my pants. He was nearly 7ft tall like High Tower out of Police Academy and built like the hulk. I thought, shit, I hope he didn't understand what I'd shouted at him the night before. We both glared at each other, then I nodded towards him with a little smile, but he didn't respond. We were both handcuffed and there were about twelve officers. I thought, thank God there's quite a few of them, as I was sure they would be needed if something went wrong.

They took us both to reception, to sign out. I signed first, and then he was at the desk. I then noticed the ape was barefoot. I thought to myself that they must have taken his shoes from him but hadn't returned them. I thought, poor fucker and wondered where he was from.

They took us out to the yard to get us transported to prison. OMG it was one of those really hot, days, I guess around 33 degrees centigrade, but in Madrid with all the city traffic and smog it felt much hotter. I was sweating like crazy.

In the yard there were about twelve policemen. The ape and me were waiting, and then a big iron van pulled up. I've seen many normal prison vans before, but this one was special. I asked one of the policemen what it was, and he told me that as the two of us were maximum risk prisoners, they weren't taking any chances. I thought, the ape looks high risk, but not me.

The van was one of the most horrible vehicles I've ever been in, and it was already so hot in there, that I wanted to get out. We were in small separate spaces with not much room to move about. I looked around and saw a small tube in the corner of the van. I was already sweating, and the heat was magnified by the van with the sun beating down on it, making us even hotter inside. I heard a big old clunking noise, as the driver started the engine. As it roared, I thought let's just get going, and I hoped it wasn't far, as I was thinking I could die in there.

We pulled out of the yard at around 1pm, the hottest part of the day. Luckily, I felt a little blast of fresh air come my way, which was heaven. I noticed that it was coming from the tube in the corner and realised it must be aircon. I felt like it was going to save my life, but it was the oldest thing I'd seen in my life.

We were now moving through the traffic, and I thought the police were wankers for moving us during siesta time. This was rush hour, and the traffic was at a snail's pace, and we were bumper to bumper. I felt as if I was deep diving and I was trying to push my head closer to the tube, so that I could breathe and feel the cold on me. It was torture, and because it was so hot outside, it was making the iron horse feel like a sauna.

We came to a halt. We didn't move for ages and I guessed they had pulled over to let the traffic clear. Then they would have a clear run to the prison. By this time, we had been in the van for well over an hour. I estimated we had only travelled a few miles.

Then the ape started in his little torture cell in the van, and I couldn't blame him. He's a big bloke and he must have sweated big time. He must have had some power as the whole van was rocking as he banged his great big King Kong paws on it.

About thirty or so minutes later, after not moving, we finally started to move, and I cheered with relief and so did the ape. Finally, we made it through the city to the outskirts, and all we wanted to do was to get out of that van. We did our last turn and now we were entering my new home the Soto de Real prison.

We pulled in and there were guards everywhere. I thought home sweet home – not. I looked closer at the sign and a shiver ran down my spine. It said 1976 the year I was born. I was thinking I was just starting my new life over again, but it was a broken life. It was weird and I was so sad.

They got us both out and hurried us into reception. They took our names, lasered our fingerprints, gave us our prison numbers, and then put us both into a holding room. This was the first time that the ape and me were in the same room and without handcuffs. I was shitting myself as I thought he could break my neck with one hand. I looked at him and thought poor fucker, as he had no footwear. I asked where he was from, but he didn't understand, so I pointed at myself, and said, 'Ingles' (English) and he replied, 'Romania,' so that was that. I looked at his bare feet and guessed he was about the same shoe size as me, size 11.

Another prisoner came in and asked if we wanted to buy anything like phonecards, coffee or smokes. I didn't smoke but I wanted one. I told him I had 3 euros, so asked if I could buy just two cigarettes and two coffees, as I was guessing the Romanian man didn't have any money. I asked if he could get size 11 trainers, flip flops, anything. He told me that the two fags were 50 cents, and the coffees were 46 cents. He also said he would look in the lost property for size 11s. I thanked him and off he went.

Within ten minutes he was back with the coffees, smokes and size 11s. I thanked him, and the Romanian looked at me puzzled, so I took one fag and one coffee, plus the flip flops and gave them to him. He shook my hand and immediately

I could feel what I had done for him meant so much. That was it, we started a friendship even with the language barrier. We managed to exchange names. His name was Mario. We hit it right off, and I thought to myself, I'd got myself a righthand man and back up. Little things go a long way as Mario was very happy.

We heard noises from the room next door, and it sounded like there were more getting checked in. Then, they began coming into the room we were in, one by one. There was two Spanish men, a Russian, and two Mexican men. They all looked mean and dangerous.

So, we were all in this room. Some were pacing and some sitting. The Mexicans were eyeing us menacingly. I could tell the Russian man didn't like them and felt uncomfortable. The Spanish men felt the same way too, I could tell. I could see Mario didn't give a fuck, and that didn't surprise me at all, as he could have killed all of us with his bare hands.

They started staring at me, and I felt uneasy, but I tried to hide my nerves. One of them called me Gringo and asked if I had any fags, as though they just expected me to hand them over. I told them I had nothing and said they should do one. I said I was here with my mate, and pointed to Mario, who immediately understood what was going on. He grinned at them and they both looked away, and that was that. I thought it was well funny. I didn't want to start fighting as I'd only just got here, but now I had the bonus of Mario as my backup.

We were in the holding room for another hour or so before the guards came and explained that they were going to take us to the starters wing for newcomers. They said we had to go in pairs as there were no single cells. They said the two Spanish could share and the same for the two Mexicans, and then pointed at Mario and the Russian and said they could share. I was the only one left and asked what would be happening to me. They told me that I'd have to wait for another prisoner to arrive, and we'd go to the starter wing when he got here.

So that was it. They led the others away. Mario and the Russian and the two Spanish said goodbye to me, but not the Mexicans. I thought here I am, alone again. Earlier in the day all I wanted to do was get away from Mario, but he was now my friend, and I felt alone and was sad to see him go.

I sat there alone for hours waiting, and my brain was thinking about everything that had gone wrong. I was also wondering who was going to be my cellmate and what they were going to be like.

After three hours, I started to hear some more checking in, and the room I was in was glass and metal, so I could see outside. I saw the guards coming with this new prisoner, who was white, and they were trying to speak with him, but he didn't understand Spanish, but I didn't think he was English either.

They were taking all his personal belongings. I noticed he had a carton of Marlborough Lights which they took but gave him one packet back. They took his wallet and counted the cash, which was over 500 euros, of which they gave him 100 euros back, and then locked the rest away. They gave him prison clothes and toiletries and took him to shower.

I waited another twenty minutes until they opened the door of the room, and the guards told me that they'd be taking us both up to our cell. He replied to them in English which was a surprise. We went down corridors and up two flights of stairs and were shown to a cell. They explained that food was coming at 7pm, and then in the morning we would get cards and prison numbers. Then we'd see a doctor and finally, we'd be able to put our money on a prison card to buy things. They shut the door on us.

The cell had bunk beds but no TV or anything else apart from a small shower. I told my cellmate which bunk I'd have, and told him my name, but said if it was easier, he could call me Luis like the Spanish do. His name was Victor, and we were friends while we were at that prison.

We began chatting and he explained he was from Georgia, near Russia and the Georgians don't like Russians. He said he was an important man, but I won't write about it here as I have the utmost respect for him. He was a top bloke who helped me out with money and fags, as I'd now started smoking, I was so stressed. I knew how bad it was for me, but it gave me a little bit of comfort for the bad times I was in.

We soon hit it off and found out that we were both Chelsea supporters, and just as spooky, we were both the same age. It was crazy, I was just a few months older than him, which was strange as he looked a lot older than me. That became clearer though when later in our talks he explained that at one point in his life, he had been a massive heroin user, and still to this day, he took medicine because of it. He showed me how all of his veins had gone. It was horrible, but the bloke was so interesting, and we spoke all night until around midnight.

CHAPTER TWENTY-SEVEN

I woke up early the next day after my first day in prison. I knew Victor wasn't awake yet. We had no curtains so I just looked out of the windows. I could see some mountains in the distance, and I thought about the Mijas mountains where I had laid my mum to rest, and my past, and my home. Now, I was in prison in Madrid, not knowing what my future held, and I was really sad.

Victor woke up. There was a lot of noise outside our cell, and then the door flew open and there were about five guards. They came in and told Victor to come with them. It was all very quick and was not done in a nice way. We nodded to each other and they slammed the cell door shut. I just thought it was normal and they were just moving us all over to the main wing.

Two hours went by and I could hear more noise, then the guards shouted out to get all my things, as I was going to the other wing, or module as it's known. I saw Mario, the Mexicans, and the other prisoners from the day before, were out in the yard, but not Victor. And I thought why did they just take him without me? I thought maybe they were flying him back to his country.

Later Victor explained that when he was taken, he saw the doctor and got his meds, and that he was given a card with a chip in it, and he said he had put all his money on this card, as when we got to the main part of the prison, there would be a shop that you could buy all sorts of things from, and phone cards. I didn't have much change left, and Mario had no money so we were fucked, but Victor said he would buy us anything we needed. What a star this man was.

Mario was called in next, and then me, so now we had all seen the doctor and got our prison cards for our money. I was worried as fuck as I needed to get someone to send me money in even though Victor would help, as I wanted my own money and to return the favour, as I don't like depending on others. We carried on walking around the exercise yard for about another two hours, waiting for the other people to be called in.

Me and Victor spent another night telling our life stories to each other. We both had mutual respect, and we swore that once it was all over and we were on the out, we would contact one another. I didn't know it would be sooner rather than later. I still wasn't sleeping well, as I was worried as fuck about what was going to happen to me, when I got back to the UK.

The next morning when I was thinking about our chats the night before I realised I'd done a lot in my lifetime, but this man was hardcore. He was an ex-military man with very close contacts in the mafia. He was tops in every way.

When the cell door opened, we were taken to get our prison cards. These can be topped up by people on the outside, and when you're broke you can use it in the prison shop. It's a much better system than in UK prisons. While we were outside waiting to get our cards, I saw Mario, and I was glad as I wanted him and Victor to meet. Victor was away getting his stuff and when he returned, he gave me a pack of Marlborough Lights, so I took five out and gave them to Mario. He gave me a hug which nearly crushed me as I don't think he knows his own strength, the big ape, ha ha!

While I was in the yard, I got talking to a 24 year-old American man, who looked nervous, so I told him to keep his head down and he'd be okay. When I asked him why he was there, he said he had flown from South America to Madrid and he was loaded. He was arrested, when he went through the x-ray machine, as he had sixty pellets of pure Cocaine inside him that he'd swallowed. He was a mule for a gang in the USA. He was lucky to be alive as I've heard of people doing that and the condoms holding the drugs bursting inside them.

He said he was in trouble where he lived as he had a massive coke problem. I was shocked when he told me he was paid 3000 euros to do this, and all the travel costs, and 500 euros to spend on the trip. He pointed out two more people in the yard that were doing the same and had come with him from the airport. They weren't with him as they were from different gangs or groups doing the same things as mules. I asked him how long he thought he would get, and he said that because it's his first time, probably 2 years.

When I noticed Victor approaching, I said goodbye to the American and wished him well. And of course, once Victor and Mario met, we were like the three amigos.

CHAPTER TWENTY-EIGHT

Well, they started taking us to our modules. This place was a massive prison with over fifteen modules, each module with two levels. It holds over one hundred and twenty prisoners.

Each prison door opened singly or altogether on electric sliding rails. Each module had a place where you could eat, and where you got your food from. There were normally four chairs per table to sit and eat, and there was a TV area. On each module was a table tennis table, and many more tables for board games and cards.

There was a shop on each module where you could buy things with your card pin number, like phone cards, chocolate, cigarettes, chips, tuna and non-alcoholic beer, and every hot drink available too, like coffees etc. So much better than UK prisons.

Outside every module was a five-a-side tarmac football pitch and two basketball grids, and more extra space for people to walk around. On the other side of the football pitch was an outside building. Inside that was a gym and small library, so plenty of things to do when you were out of your cell. Also, there was a medical hatch to collect your meds every morning between each module.

The guards were placed in turret style buildings which looked down onto the courtyard. They would watch the prisoners through the TV monitors and could see every move you made. They would rarely come into the courtyard unless there was trouble. If they needed anybody, they would shout your name on a loudspeaker and you would have to go to the main entrance straight away to find out what they wanted.

So, there we were, getting split up to go our different ways to our modules, and they shouted my name out, and said I was to go to module 8. Mario was to go to a different module, so he and I got separated. I quickly said goodbye to him, but from that day on, I never got to see him again. I thought this was sad and I hoped he had a good future and a better life ahead.

So here we go again. This was going to be my new home. I didn't know anybody, and I had no idea how long I would be there for. Welcome to module 8 I said to myself, as I entered it with the others. And you get this weird sense that it's all happening. You're the new ones and all eyes are on you.

Another inmate came up to us, and his job was to show us about and take us to our new cells. I was on level one. When I got to my new cell my new cellmate wasn't there. He was probably downstairs or out on the yard. I wondered who it was and hoped that he and I would get on and be friends.

I unpacked and noticed he had the bottom bunk, but I was happy to have the top bunk, so all was good there. There was a small shower, a table, a chair, and a window with a nice view looking at the mountains, and we had a television. Home sweet home, I thought. I unpacked and was ready to go and mingle, and have a good look about to see if I could find anybody English.

I was very sad wandering around but trying not to show my emotions. You have to be on your guard at all times. I was feeling shit. I had little money. Victor was gone, and now Mario, and my family in the UK didn't even know if I was okay, or even where I was. For the first time it just hit me. I felt so alone it was horrible.

I entered the outside building into the library, and said to the inmate worker there, 'Are there any English people on module 8?' He pointed to one man sitting down reading a book, and told me he was Irish, so that was it. I went up to say hello.

He was a medium sized, stocky man and looked like he enjoyed his work-outs. We exchanged names. His name was Damian, and he was 25 years old, and was from Limerick. We decided to continue our chat outside walking around the yard. He explained that he was in trouble back in Ireland for threatening to kill someone, and he had been inside for these allegations before. He had already been in Soto del Real for three weeks at this point and was waiting to be sent back to Ireland.

I explained my situation as we carried on chatting, and we started to become friends. I was telling him I'd travelled to Dublin on many occasions with parties and drinking, which is quite normal in Ireland, and how I had gone to the most famous Temple bar where I had seen Colin Farrell the movie star in there. One of my other trips was down to Cork in the South, where I loved walking on some of the best beaches in Ireland, and I thought it was a wonderful place.

I told him my nickname L.O.T.D. and he laughed his head off and thought it was great, and he loved the song Lord of the Dance, and I said I'd met Michael Flatley for real on one occasion when he was doing one of his shows. Damian and me hit it right off and walked around the yard chatting for another hour or so.

The alarm went off. This was the sign for dinner as it was 6pm, and so he offered me to go and get my dinner with him and sit on the normal table where he ate his. There I met his cellmate, who was an American who was in for smuggling tons of hash out of Spain to America. He was doing quite a long sentence but was a really nice guy. This was the same guy in the library who had told me about Damian. He spoke fluent Spanish and English, and if you wanted any help with paperwork, he was happy to fill it out and translate. So, that was it. I'd met two new friends in here already.

When we had finished our dinner, the shop had opened. It opened three times a day, morning, lunchtime and after dinner. You could buy anything you wanted to take to your cell for the night. Damian bought me a coffee and some chocolate. Then the alarm went off for everybody to go upstairs to their cells to be locked up for the night. I thanked him and said that we would catch up again the following day for a walk.

I got upstairs and went to my cell. Now was the time to meet my new cellmate. I entered and saw a short stocky man there, so I said, 'Hola', and then 'Hello'. He told me his name was Carlos and he was from Colombia. He lived in Garlica he said, in the North of Spain with his Colombian wife and kids. He didn't speak English at all, so we spoke in Spanish.

I was telling him about my life and my family too, and how much I loved South America, and I had a partner who was from Colombia, and I had visited there and spent quite a bit of time in South America. I told him that I loved his country and thought it was beautiful. I also told him I'd spent a lot of time in Panama and would like to live there one day. I explained why I was in prison, and he did too. He was connected to some regions back in Colombia with the Colombian cartels. He was caught with six kilos of Cocaine and was doing a six-year sentence for it, but he didn't have much time inside left.

We got to know each other more and more as we talked, and we hit if right off and became very good friends. We still remain friends today and will be meeting in the future.

Every night, which I thought was funny, Monday to Friday at 8pm, Carlos loved a South American programme which was on TV. It was a bit like our EastEnders back home, but this one was a very dramatic and romantic sitcom, and all the female stars looked like porn stars. They all had boob jobs and were ever so beautiful. It was amazing. But Carlos sometimes got quite upset watching it, especially the romantic parts, and that's what I thought was so funny: a big Colombian man with his background and what he was in for being upset over a programme. I thought that was hilarious. In time I got hooked to it myself!

Carlos said he was a Madrid fan, and I told him I was a Malaga fan and went to the games. If any of the football games came on the TV, we would watch together and get a load of non-alcoholic beers from the shop downstairs, and we would have a right good night.

Carlos also had a tattoo gun in our cell and would sometimes do people a tattoo. I could see and tell that nobody messed with him. He was high up the levels in ranking and everybody spoke to him with respect and honour. Most of the time when we were out of the cell and downstairs, Carlos would sit at his normal table and chair and play poker with some of the other players in module 8, mainly more Colombians and Russians.

One day he asked me to join them and play, but I soon realised the stakes were too high, and refused politely. There was some big money going on these games, but without fail he would play and be at that table every day. You could tell whether he had won or lost by his mood swings when he went upstairs, but he was always great with me and we respected each other. If I had any problems with anything or anyone, he was there.

Most of the days I spent walking around the yard with Damian, doing pot shots from a distance to the basketball netting. One afternoon, I was walking around with him in the yard, and I heard my name L.O.T.D. shouted out. I looked around and it was two of my friends that I knew from Morocco. It was great to see them, as we had been out many nights before in Tangier in one of the famous clubs there called 555, and out and about in Fuengirola on some occasions.

They couldn't believe they were seeing me in there. I explained why I was there, and they said I should have nothing to worry about. I knew without asking what they were in for. I knew it was smuggling hash into Spain. I knew the family very well. I told them I didn't have much money, so they took me to the shop and bought me toiletries, drinks and anything else I wanted, and I was happy. It made my day, and theirs for seeing me!

CHAPTER TWENTY-NINE

A couple of weeks had passed, and I had become very good friends with a man from Syria. Every day we walked and chatted about life. He had moved to Holland about twelve years earlier, because of how dangerous his homeland was. He had seen his uncle murdered in front of him, and he had to flee and escape his home country, and he now had a new life in Holland.

He was very clever and spoke Dutch and English well. He had a son with a Dutch lady, and he had fallen on hard times when he split up with her. He had no work so he decided to work with a Dutch firm importing hash out of Spain into Holland. He was moving a two-ton hash shipment onto a boat ready to leave for Holland, when he was caught with the group and got a two-year sentence.

As we were chatting one day, he told me this story about an internet shop in Amsterdam. He was upset when he heard two ladies chatting about his country and dissing his people for coming to Holland and nicking all their jobs, and mixing races with their own kind. He was so upset that he spoke to them angrily. They didn't realise that he spoke Dutch and could understand everything they were talking about. He told them many people had died in his country and he hadn't wanted to leave his country, but he had been forced to so he didn't end up dead, like hundreds of thousands have.

They chatted back to him really badly. They said they didn't care and told him to get out of their country. He was dirty racist scum, like gypsies, and made mess everywhere. The lady ordered him out of her internet shop. He left upset and angry. I told him that I would have reacted the same as him, and that it was terrible the way he'd been treated. He was walking away from the shop still feeling angry and upset, and thinking how dare they be so rude to him and talk about his people like that. He wanted revenge, so he told me he went to a fruit and veg shop. I was thinking what the fuck for. He said he bought two potatoes, and I was thinking what the fuck? Have you lost it?? What the fuck do you want two potatoes for? He explained to me he got back around the corner and headed for the internet shop. He opened the front door of the shop, and the two ladies and everybody else who had seen the argument that had just happened, saw him.

He shouted, 'Bitches!' They shouted back at him, and then he shouted, 'For the name of my people, now it's time for you all to die in hell.' They all looked at him worried and frightened, as he put both of the potatoes close to his mouth and made the action of pulling a pin out of a grenade, and then rolled them into the shop.

Everybody ducked and jumped onto the floor, screaming and shouting for their lives. He just casually walked up the road with a smile on his face. It must have taken them a little while to realise it was fake, but I'm sure it took the wind out of their sails. I could not stop laughing. But then I told him he was lucky he had not been arrested as it was a terrorist threat. In the UK he might have got five to ten years. He shrugged his shoulders and said he didn't care. It was for him and his people.

Another week had passed, and Damian had left and gone back to Ireland, and I was wondering when it was my turn. I sat there in the yard and looked at the sky and could see the flight paths of the planes heading for South America and the USA. I knew Madrid Airport was close by, and for some reason I was just wishing I was on one of those planes going on holiday somewhere, but now there was no chance of that. I didn't even know how long I would be here, and I didn't know what would happen in the UK. I was feeling down, tired and sad and just wishing this nightmare was over.

Many nights and days passed, and I didn't seem to be going anywhere. I enjoyed the days out in the yard in the sun, and the nights in the cell watching the romantic TV programme with Carlos, but his was no life to what I'd had before I got messed up in all this shit. Things just weren't moving fast enough, and the days were long. To be honest, all you do is keep thinking and wandering around like a lost person, and thinking of your family and friends, and my beloved dogs and my home, good home cooked food, restaurants, bars and girls. Now that was all taken away.

I was sitting in the yard on the floor one day in a zombie state, just staring into thin air and thinking, and then I heard my name called out on the loudspeaker, 'Hombre senor Wright.'

'Mr Wright can you please come to the main entrance' is what they were saying. My heart started pounding. Was this my time to go? I jumped up and rushed as fast as I could to get to the main entrance where they wanted me.

The man at the entrance was waiting for me with two other guards. They asked me to follow them. We went to an office in another part of the prison. I was just thinking I was there to get my paperwork to start my trip to the UK, to find out my doom or get released.

I was waiting in the office when another prisoner turned up with a guard. He was white about my height, and then another two prisoners turned up. One of them was small and looked like he was from Chile, South America, and the other bloke was black, probably Afro Caribbean. I was puzzled and said to one of the guards, 'What's bloody going on here, why are we all here?'

The guard pointed to me and the man I thought was from Chile, and the black man, and said, 'Don't worry it's not your problem. It's this man here.' He pointed to the white man. 'It's his problem, and you lot are here just to do a line up for an ID parade on webcam. The victim is going to be looking at all of you and pointing out the culprit.'

I was like, What the fuck! The poor prick has no chance. Or was I going to be his saviour?

The man from Chile was brown and small and the other was a black man, so they certainly weren't giving the man a good chance. I laughed to myself and thought they were taking the piss. Anyway, the white man was from Russia, and he was nervous as hell and I couldn't blame him. I was his only chance. He had been a cat burglar on big posh villas, robbing them for their money and jewellery.

There was a lady at the back of the room looking at us all through the webcam. I was number 3, the Russian was number 1, the Chilean was number 2 and the African man was number 4. The guard shouted out to the webcam, 'Is there any man here you want to walk closer to the webcam, off the line towards you?'

Straight away the lady picked out number 1, for him to step forward two steps, so he did. Then she said number 3. Well, that was me, so I stepped two steps forward. I could see number 1 next to me, so nervous he couldn't keep still, and you could tell he was guilty as hell, so I tried to help him by fidgeting myself and trying to look uncomfortable too. But to be honest I hate burglars and have no time for them.

A couple of minutes passed. That probably seemed like forever for him. Then the lady said number 3 step back to your line. So that was me back, which just left him. She asked the guard for number 1 to move much closer to the webcam so she could see him clearly. Anyway, he did, then she asked him to turn all the way around, which he did, then the lady shouted to the guard, 'Thank you. That's all I need.' She sounded very upset, and you can't blame her. She'd just seen the man who had entered her private space, her home. The guard turned off the webcam and told us four to leave the room and wait outside.

Once outside the white Russian man seemed happy, for what I don't know. He spoke good English and he came up to me, and said, 'How do you think I got on?' Well, I just pissed myself, when he asked, 'Do you think she's going to say it was me?' I thought to myself, are you smoking crack mate? Of course, she recognised you, look at the other two here, you had no chance, as I was your only chance.

Then he asked, 'What do you think?'

I couldn't' hold back. I didn't want to give him false hope, and I said, 'Look mate, you're fucked.'

MINISTERIO DE INTERIOR

SECRETARIA GENERAL DE INSTITUCIONES PENITENCIARIAS
CENTRO PENITENCIARIO DE MADRID V

EJEMPLAR: INTERNO

De conformidad con lo previsto en el artículo 75/1 del R.P., esta Dirección, en uso de las atribuciones conferidas en el art. 280/2-5° de la misma norma, acuerda la aplicación al/la interno/a de este Establecimiento

INTERNO: LLOYD WRIGH (NIS 2016013616)

de las siguientes **limitaciones regimentales**:

X	Permanencia en celda individual del módulo 15
X	Disfrute de un mínimo de tres horas de patio

Este acuerdo se ha adoptado para garantizar la seguridad y el buen orden del Centro en base a naturaleza y gravedad de los delitos presuntamente cometidos y datos obrantes en su expediente.

Su situación será revisada por la Junta de Tratamiento a efectos de una posible reconsideración de grado de Tratamiento o en su caso régimen de vida aplicable.

La adopción del presente acuerdo se participará al Juzgado Central de Vigilancia Penitenciaria de Madrid, asistiéndole el derecho a recurrir el presente acuerdo en queja según lo previsto en el art. 76.2 apartado g) de la L.O.G.P.

En Soto del Real (Madrid), a 24 de Octubre 2016.

EL DIRECTOR

Recibí copia fecha:
El Interno/a,

Entregué F°:

CARRETERA M-609
KM 3.500
C.P. 28971 SOTO DEL REAL

CHAPTER THIRTY

The days went past, and I tried my best to occupy my time, but time never went very quickly. Out of the blue, the speaker went again with my name, so I rushed to the entrance.

Finally, I thought this was my time. My spirits were high, as I thought it couldn't be another ID parade again. I can't be that unlucky. I got to the entrance again, and the guard said, 'Go pack your stuff you're coming with me.' Yippee I thought, things are starting to move. I just want to get to the UK to sort this mess out. I was buzzing. I wanted to say goodbye to Carlos, but the guard said no, and that I had to get my stuff and come now.

I got back to the entrance with all my things, and there were about eight guards there waiting for me. I thought it was a bit odd and asked why there was so many of them, and where was I going. He told me I was now going to the seg, which is otherwise known as module 15. I was like, 'What? You're joking.'

I thought it was a prison joke before everyone gets to leave. They said that it was no joke, and that I was a dangerous man who couldn't remain in the main population, with any others. They told me I couldn't mix with anyone, as I was on the TV news and on the radio, and I was one of Europe's most wanted, and one of the UKs most wanted, and I was head of an organised crime group.

I was like, 'What the fuck, are you 007 or something? What are you going on about?' But this was no joke, and this was happening to me. Here we go again! All a little bit much, wasn't it?

Well, you can imagine I was as worried as fuck. They marched me down to the seg like military. All of them were heavy duty. We got to the seg reception and they took all my stuff off me and took me to my cold bleak cell, barefoot. It was a joke, and inhumane.

I entered what was going to be my new home, again not knowing how long I would be in there. There was no TV, no nothing. A light on the ceiling that stayed on, and the tap kept dripping. This was not the seg. This was mental and physical damage. This would surely break anyone, and when you looked out of the small window, three feet outside this window was another wall, so you were really looking out at fuck all. It was so cold and damp in there. It was horrible. Time defo stands still here.

The only movement in the cell was a cockroach. Three hours later they brought me a few of my things in a plastic bag. I started to unpack what little I had. I felt so low. I had never felt like this before. This was like life had ended. To make things worse they only gave me one of my flip flops back, as if the cell wasn't bad enough.

They were trying to break me. Next, I pulled out my toothbrush, and they had snapped it in half. Bastards, I thought, why? I pressed the bell, and the guard came, and I showed him the toothbrush and told him they'd snapped it. He said that they'd snapped it because they thought I might attack them with it. What a joke! I mentioned my other flip flop, and he just laughed at me, pushed the shutter down and walked off. I thought to myself, this is going to drive me crazy. I tried to get some sleep, but with the tap dripping, the noise from this and the light being on, it was pure torture, and I was thinking about what he said, being Europe's and the UK's most wanted. I lay on the bed for quite some time with my head just spinning with crazy thoughts, and then I wondered if there was anybody else there, so I started to shout out hola and hello repeatedly and asking whether there was anybody else down here.

To my surprise somebody answered back, and in English. Oh my God, it was Victor, my friend from Georgia. Like I said earlier, we would meet sooner rather than later. Wow, it was such a buzz knowing that I was not alone, and of course it was my friend. I was so happy somehow, and in this bad situation it gave me a lift. All of a sudden, I didn't feel so down.

Victor said he was two cells down, and he'd been in there since he left me in the starters wing. I was like, 'Shit mate, so sorry to hear that.'

I told him everything I'd been through, and how they had come and got me and brought me here. He just couldn't' believe it, and I told him what they were saying about me. We spent ages talking and we were up till late, and he then said that we would be allowed out the following morning for an hour, and the same every morning in this small yard. He also said there is a small shopping trolley coming around from the prison shop. He asked if I needed anything and said he would get me whatever I wanted and told me not to worry about money as he had plenty. I thanked him and told him we would talk in the morning.

I woke up the next morning after a shit night's sleep, with the fucking tap, drip, drip, drip, which was making me go around the bend. I shouted out good morning to Victor and he replied.

We were now out in the yard, and it was great to see him, but I could tell and see that seg had taken its toll on him, as he was so white from seeing no sunlight down there, and he looked horribly stressed, but we were so pleased and happy to see each other that it made our spirits high.

The yard was very small, and we had two guards watching our every move in this tiny, bleak yard. Above our heads was netting to stop helicopters coming in to rescue or to make a great escape or drop anything in towards us. This seg and yard was like a prison for terrorists, and it was hardcore. Even the guards were holding weapons.

Another man entered the yard. He was Italian. Victor introduced me to him, but I can't remember his name. He had been down here the longest, and he looked frail, weak and extremely white. He smoked like a chimney. We all talked for a while and the trolley turned up and we all had drinks and snacks. Victor was a pure gem.

They called us bang on the hour and made us go back into our cells. The next morning, I received a package from the British Embassy, with lots to read. I thought at least they know I'm in here, so they must be doing something for me. Every day is extremely long in here, and I swear boredom is a killer.

I heard a noise outside my cell, and the shutter was still down as I'd received my dinner twenty minutes before. I looked out and there was this prison cleaner. He was a trans op bloke, with a massive pair of tits. I started talking to he or she, with he or she replying they were from Brazil and in for drug smuggling. She asked me for a fag and said I could have a feel of her tits if I gave her a few fags. I was like, 'What the fuck! You can fuck off, but you can have a couple anyway for nothing.'

All of a sudden, I heard Victor roaring with laughter, and he said she'd done the same with him and we both laughed out loud.

I said to him, 'Oh my God, this place is crazy, get me out of here. I bet you had a squeeze, with a pull off.'

He replied, laughing, 'Fuck off.'

A few days had passed. They were long, very long days. Time really does stand still, and all you can do is think, and that sometimes makes you go mad as you overthink, and your mind starts playing tricks on you. I was even starting to talk to myself out loud. Was I really going insane?

But yes, at last I was woken early by the guard banging my door. He said, 'Get your things, you're going to the UK.' This was finally it. I had to pinch myself to make sure I really was awake, and it wasn't a dream.

Victor heard too, and I shouted, 'Yes, it's my time, my friend.' He wished me the best of luck and said we would defo meet one day on the outside. We were talking before about me coming to Georgia, and he said I was welcome to come and stay with his family whenever I wanted. I was sad to leave him in this crazy inhuman pit. I wished him all the best.

Anyway, I waited over an hour for them to come and get me. What the fuck did they think I was packing? I only had a broken toothbrush, a damp towel and one flip flop. I packed all this in one minute, so I thought to myself they are pricks. Before I left the cell, I wrote on the wall *LOTD was here 2016 England.*

They took me to the main entrance of the prison, the first place I entered when I came in. They gave me my man bag and my personal belongings which wasn't much at all. Then, they took me outside to a prison van, and there was a police car there full of Guardia Civil policemen, to escort the prison van to the airport. It was all a bit too much again, I thought.

Luckily the airport wasn't far, a thirty-minute drive. I'd flown out of this airport on many occasions to many countries around the world, but this was going to be my first flight to the UK from Madrid. It just seemed weird, and I was to be handcuffed and escorted all the way.

We made it inside to the police department area of the airport, and they took me to this cell, and told me we were waiting for the English police to come and receive me, and I would be in their hands then. They opened the cell, and I went in. It was a massive cell which held up to twenty-five people and there were two people inside already, but they were sleeping right at the back. I just put my back on the wall and sat there quietly.

About an hour went past and the door opened, and the airport police brought a young man to be put in with us. He looked so nervous and was in his early twenties. In the back of my mind, it clicked. I thought about the young man back in the starters wing yard, when I was back in prison. The young man with drug pellets inside his body. Sure enough I was right. As we started talking, he said he was Spanish, and he was coming back from Venezuela.

Within a couple of hours, the door opened, and they told me the English police were here, and told me to come to the office where they were. I entered the office, and they had sent three policemen who were all well over 40 years old and looked like computer nerds. I thought what happened to the high security that the Spanish had given me on the way up to this point. No offence, boys, but I thought in the back of my head, one looked like Penfold out of Dangermouse, and one looked like Wally out of where's Wally in the comic mags, and one looked like Mike Gatting, the cricket man, but with glasses on. They said their hellos, and said their job was just to return me to the UK and they didn't want any trouble, and that all should go smoothly. They said that they didn't know anything about my case and were just there to transport me back.

I asked, 'When are we going?' They said, 'We are booked on the next flight out of here with British Airways to London Heathrow Airport, and we will be at the back of the plane, and you will be in the middle of two of us and will be wearing special handcuffs for travelling.' They said I would be able to still eat and drink with these handcuffs, and another set will handcuff me to one of them.

For some strange reason, I pictured myself as David Blaine and I had just escaped the handcuffs and them and was jumping out of the plane with a parachute! Ha ha, wake up, LOTD!

So, we boarded the plane and with handcuffs on, you can imagine, everybody stares at you. The cabin crew were there to greet us, and two of them were fit as fuck, and you know me, I'm a sucker for an air stewardess, so I gave them a little LOTD wink.

As they could see, I was in the presence of three policemen, and with my handcuffs on. All the girls love a bad boy. One of them gave me a beautiful smile, and my thinking overpowered me yet again. I was thinking if these three policemen weren't about, me and her would be getting it on in the toilet and joining the mile high club, ha ha.

So, we were into the flight, and one of the policemen asked if I would like a drink. I replied, 'A large Gin and Tonic please.'

He replied, 'Don't take the piss Wrighty.'

Well, you gotta try, the man above loves a trier. The air stewardesses brought us snacks. The copper next to me opened a pack of nuts, and I said, 'Are you lot stupid?' He looked puzzled, and I said, 'Haven't you done your homework on me? I'm allergic to nuts?'

He went bright red, and I said, 'Got you there, didn't I!' and laughed, but he wasn't impressed.

We just passed the Isle of Wight and we were starting our descent. The seat belt lights flicked on and off. My heart started to jump. I was excited and anxious about what they had planned for me, and my road ahead. We landed, and as soon as we touched down, the copper said to me, 'Mr Wright, now we are on UK turf, we have arrested you for conspiracy to supply Cocaine A, and conspiracy to supply hash B.'

I was like, 'I thought you said you knew nothing about my case. My arse, you lot talk bollocks.' But in all fairness, they were only doing their job and they were okay with me on our journey.

To be honest, the journey and what I'd been through up until now, had been a nightmare. It was challenging, physically and mentally, so draining and damaging. I thought to myself shit, I've gone so far, police cars, police vans, the iron horse and now aeroplanes. I was thinking of the movie *Planes, Trains and Automobiles*, and was thinking fuck, now all I needed was a train ride!

Now, I was back on British soil, and I hadn't lived here for over 16 years. Of course, I'd been back in those years, but only for weekends to see my kids and my granddaughter, to take them out for meals and shopping, and great family moments. This time, I didn't know how long I would be here for.

CHAPTER THIRTY-ONE

I know I'm British, but my homeland is not for me to live in. To come and go again is enough for me. I was thinking what was going to be the outcome, and how long would I really have to stay here for, and would it be prison, and how long would that be for? I was homesick already and I just wished I was on a return flight back to Spain.

We were now in the airport and everybody was staring at me with my handcuffs on with the three policemen. Then more police turned up in uniforms, and whenever you're arrested, you still have to go through passport control, but without the queueing. You go through the passport control where all the pilots and air stewardesses go.

We got to our turn and the police got my paperwork out that the Spanish gave them, and they didn't realise that I didn't have my passport included. They must have thought it would be there, and now there was a big problem. It was quite funny really, as they didn't know what to do, as passport control wouldn't let us through. I was hoping maybe this is my chance of a return flight. But I couldn't be that lucky!

After twenty minutes of calls and lots of talking through their radios, a man turned up with some paperwork. I had to sign, and we were clear to go. They took me out of the airport, and into a police van, and straight to the local airport police station. I think it was the Metropolitan Police. They put me in the cells there for a couple of hours, while they sorted more paperwork out. Then they said they would be taking me to Reading police station.

When we arrived at Reading, they signed me in. They let me have a phone call. It was like heaven. I rang my daughter and told her what I'd been through. She was upset and shocked, but was happy to hear my voice. I told her I didn't want her to worry as she was heavily pregnant with my second granddaughter. I sent my love to all and said that I would be back in touch very soon.

She replied, 'Be strong Dad, all will be okay, and we are here for you with lots of love.'

Then I thought to myself, one good thing about being in the UK was that my kids live here, so I was looking forward to lots of visits. Secondly, the police doctor came to see me, and I said, 'Oh my God, where did they get you from.'

She was a super fit little blonde lady around twenty-five years old. She really was a nice caring character, and we had a little chat, and she gave me the all-clear on my medical check-up.

I spent two nights in Reading police station, and I thought wow, things have changed. You can press the bell, and a friendly person comes with food and drinks. I couldn't remember that 20 years ago, when I was arrested for a personal little bit of hash.

Because I was arrested on a European arrest warrant, the UK police were not allowed to interview me, and they still haven't up to this day, as the courts and the lawyers have to deal with it all through the court. Anyway, I ended up going to Reading Magistrates Court first. I didn't have a lawyer but there was a man next to me in the cell, in the downstairs courtrooms, and I asked whether I could use his lawyer, which I did end up doing.

He advised me that because I was on a conspiracy for supplying Cocaine A, that I would not get bail, and he told me not to plead today, as it was too early to put in a plea without somebody looking into it properly. He needed to make himself familiar with the case and all its paperwork. He said he would let the judge know that he needed time to do this.

In the courtroom, the judge said that this was a matter for the High Courts, as they were very serious allegations, and the judge put me on remand, and he was going to advise the High Court that further proceedings were necessary.

As I left the courtroom, a lawyer came up to me. Her name was Heather Howe, and she was to become my new lawyer, and up to today we are good, close friends. I think she's a fantastic lady and a super lawyer.

So that was it. I was sent to prison on remand. To be honest, my dreams were just crushed. I felt sad, as I thought I would have got bail.

I arrived at Bullingdon HMP Prison, which is a B/C Cat prison. I hadn't a clue really where I was, until another lad told me we were only seven miles from Bicester Shopping Village. I remembered coming here twenty odd years ago, for some designer clothes shopping, so we were in Oxfordshire.

They checked us in and took our photos, and did medical checks, and gave me my prison number. This number stays with you for life, they told me, A5242DW. I thought what do you mean life? As soon as I'm done in here, I don't ever want to come back, so this number to me, is just a part of my life, and one I really don't want to have, thank you.

That was that. They moved us from the reception area to the starters wing, which is called F1, where they put all the first-time prisoners before they split you all up, and move you over onto the other main population of all the other wings.

So, there I was on F1. I had a single cell, and the toilet was filthy. The whole wing smelt of shit and different odours. It was terrible and people were banging and shouting, and everyone was pressing the bell on the alarms in their cells.

This was nothing like the prison in Spain. It was so different. These people in here had problems. I soon came to realise when we were all let out of our cells, and there were about eighty of them, that more than half the inmates rushed to the medical hatch to collect their meds. Most have crack Cocaine and heroin problems.

I thought to myself, oh my God, what has England come to? Get me out of this hellhole. Back in the Spanish prison, every morning, out of the one hundred and twenty inmates on my module, only three people had a drug problem and went to the medical hatch. Here in the UK, they have a massive problem.

It was so shocking seeing how people were and what hard drugs had done to them, absolutely terrible. Some people were so thin, with little hair and no teeth, and looking so much older than their age. The whole place was such a mess, it was like being inside a horror movie. I felt so uncomfortable and dirty in there, and I just wanted out. I was in shock to be honest, but I had to be strong, and this was my new home.

After the shock had settled, and a few days had passed, and I'm not going to lie, they were tough, but like in any environment, you learn to deal with it. Well, you have to. You can't just walk up to the guard, and say, 'Excuse me but I've had enough now. Can you please let me go,' and the door just opens. This is what prisons are about. You need to get your head down and do your time, but it's a lot harder for some people with drug problems and mental health issues. And some of these inmates have grown up with these issues. It's a tough and horrible place sometimes, the world.

I soon heard that I had co-defendants in here, who were part of the same case as mine, but all had been sentenced. Their sentences ranged from 19 years maximum, down to 3 years. I didn't know any of them, except for one, but I hadn't seen that fellow for over 15 years. And obviously I also knew the one that I dropped the money to. So, that was it, I was on remand and waiting to go to court, and now I had to settle into my new life.

About five days had passed, and I met this man who was two cells down. To me he looked to be in his late forties. His name was Michael, and he seemed nice and polite and talked very openly with me, so we became very good friends, and we swapped our newspapers. We would walk together in the exercise yard and have our daily chats. I learned that Michael was in prison for murder, and I thought to myself, well, I am in prison so I will come across these people in here for these types of crimes. This is normal everyday prison life really, but I'm only in here to do my time and get out. What other people have done is their business.

We spent more and more time together on our walks, and he had just received a thirty-three-year life sentence for this murder, and he was called the Wind in the Willows killer. At the time I didn't think much about this, as I had a lot on my mind, and my head was screwed with my own thoughts, and what was going on in my own life. When you're in prison, people tell you all sorts of stories, and you don't know what is real and what is not.

On another day when I was walking in the yard with him, he was telling me more, about how he had stalked Kate Moss, and taken photographs of her wherever she was. I thought it was all a bit weird, and just chit chat. I thought he had made it all up and didn't think much of it. I couldn't believe it, three months down the line when an advert came up on the TV about a programme about the Wind in the Willows killer, and it showed a photo of Michael, and explained how he had repeatedly stabbed the victim thirty-three times. The reason for the stabbing was a rare Wind in the Willows book, which was worth seventy thousand pounds. I thought oh my God, I've got to watch this.

I did watch it, and I couldn't believe it was Michael, as it was absolutely brutal, what happened. It's no surprise that he got the sentence he got. On the programme it also said about him stalking Kate Moss, and I was like, shit, he was telling the truth after all, and I went into total shock after the programme.

I was still on F1 starters wing, and for the first week, every inmate had to have default food, which is vegetarian food only, no meat. All I could remember was that like everybody else, I couldn't stop farting, and you can imagine the smell on the wing! Finally, after twelve days, they told me to get ready, as I was moving to B wing, which is in the main part of the prison.

I got to B wing, and this was called the detox wing. With the prison system being at full capacity, I ended up there even though I didn't need detox. The meds hatch on this wing was rammed every morning and afternoon. This wing was like something out of Shaun of the Dead. There were some really fucked up people walking about like zombies.

I did have a bit of luck when I came to B wing though, as they moved me into a big double cell, with a young lad from Aldershot, named James. He was in for drug charges too. To be honest, most of the prison population are in for drugs, which is overwhelming the prison system.

To my disbelief, on this wing I would hear shouts and screams of *man down* and the alarm would go off, and the medical team would come racing to the wing. 'Man down' means an inmate is having a spice attack, and is normally fitting on the floor. Seeing this, I was very concerned and shocked. I never knew much about spice or rice or these illegal highs. In Spain these hardly exist, and I'd never heard of them. They were definitely not in the Spanish prison system, but it was a big problem here. Even more horrific was that people would stand and clap and laugh at the people having fits. Sooner or later, someone is going to die from this. It's absolutely horrible and a drain on the prison, the screws and the fantastic medical teams.

I remember in the weeks leading up to Xmas, within one week, there were five men down, and three of them went down in the same afternoon. You have to be careful if you smoke, as if you run out of your own baccy and ask someone for a roll up, they will spike your roll up. It's that crazy, so you should just smoke your own.

I remember one afternoon they spiked this Indian man, and he was fitting out big style. They took him to the shower to drain him off. Luckily that stopped him from fitting more, as he was going into a very bad state. It was an absolute joke, as he looked so confused and scared. I went to see if he was alright, as I felt sorry for him. Thankfully, he was coming round, but was in shock, bless him.

The food was a lot better now as I was getting meat, and I was getting visits to the library. It was amazing to have access to books. Here, I met one of my best buddies, Richard, who worked there. Also, while down in the library, the team there were especially helpful. There was Dawn and Alison, and they helped me with this book that I'm writing. I told them that one day, when I'm out and my book takes off, I would come back to Bullingdon as a visitor to personally sign copies, and of course hand a few over for the prison library, so the inmates can read them.

CHAPTER THIRTY-TWO

I was lucky again the first week of being on B wing, as I landed a job in industrial cleaning.

Most of the days at work we would be training on all types of equipment, and going about the prison, cleaning different parts. One of our main cleaning jobs was picking up litter from outside the wings, so I got to get outside the prison walls on a daily basis. The rubbish was a massive problem, as people were chucking it out of their windows. On some occasions, we would find handmade blades, and small mars bar mobile phones, and sometimes drugs.

So now I was working and trying to make the time go as good for me as possible, and I was reading lots of books from the prison library, while waiting for my lawyer Heather Howe to come and see me about my case.

Just before Xmas I received one hundred pounds from my brother, and it gave me a big lift. I thought maybe he does have a bit of a heart, and is thinking of me, but this notion was short lived. When I rang him to say thanks, he smugly told me the money wasn't from him. It was from my friend Norm. What a joke, and a waste of a phone call that I made. It was almost as though he enjoyed letting me know that he would not have sent me anything.

I received a letter from Heather, saying when she was coming to see me which cheered me up, as I hoped I would get to know a bit more about what was going on with my case. I explained to her that I had picked some money up once from a car. It was for the sale of some weed which wasn't mine, and nor was the money. I was just asked if I could do it while I was over in the UK seeing my kids. I was picking it up for the lads in Hull, and I was going to send it up to them, or they would come down and collect it, and that was the only part I played in this.

She showed me the case paperwork and told me that the car I picked up the money from was bugged by the NCA, and she explained to me that in the car where I was picking the money up from, the man had offered me a kilo of Cocaine. To be honest, I couldn't remember this as I was only there to pick the money up, and I didn't reply to his offer, as I simply wasn't interested. I made no comment at all when he offered it to me.

She explained that was why there was a charge of conspiracy to supply Cocaine. I was like, oh my God, I can't believe this is happening to me, and I swallowed and felt very uneasy, and not well at all. She said that the charge was very serious and would lead to a heavy sentence.

Straight away, I said, 'NO, NO, NO. This is nothing to do with me at all.'

I learnt that all the other co-defendants were done for conspiracy to supply Cocaine, but I was definitely and truly not involved in this and I was going for a not guilty plea on this charge. I admitted that I was guilty of picking money up for the sale of some weed.

Heather advised me that the conspiracy charge for the Cocaine was weak, and that my barrister would deal with this, so I was definitely pleading not guilty. As for the money for the weed, I would plead guilty on part of the sale of it, seeing as I was there to pick the money up. She advised me, that with the early guilty pleas for the sale of the weed, I would get full credit of thirty three percent off my whole sentence if I got one.

I stayed on remand and waited for the court date.

My whole life had been shattered, and I could not stop thinking about it all, and this stupid Cocaine charge I had on me. I was advised that I could be looking at a 10 to 14 year sentence, if they charged me with the weed and the Cocaine. I was in a right mess, but Heather was hopeful that the Cocaine charge would be dropped, and that I would only get done for the supply of the weed, which she admitted was bad enough anyway. She tried to reassure me and said that the barrister would do his very best for me, and she would be back in touch.

The next few weeks were long. I was shattered with the worry and stress of it all. I was not sleeping, and it took a massive toll on me. I was so low I had to see the doctor, and he placed me on anxiety tablets. Also, I was having a problem with my scalp as I was scratching it all the time due to the stress, which caused my head to go red, and the skin to become dry. It was horrible. As you can imagine, I was totally stressed out.

Then at last I received some good news in my life. My daughter had just given birth to my granddaughter. She was a good weight, and both were healthy, so I was over the moon that I was a grandfather again. I was well happy.

I'd just met another man inside, and we had become mates. We are still in contact today. His name is Pete, but I refer to him as pistol Pete. One day he was driving his van down the road, and he turned left at the traffic lights, unaware that his left indicator wasn't working, and there was a police car behind him. The police flashed him to pull over.

Pete was a bit nervous, and the police could tell this, and asked to search the van. Down in the footwell of his van, they found a sawn-off shotgun. So that was it. He was nicked. Even the copper was in shock finding this when they'd only stopped him for a light not working. Pete told them that he was getting rid of it and was on his way to dump it in the canal. The police found out more about Pete, who was a builder. He didn't get paid for a big job he had worked on, and he was having problems with his client, and he wasn't far from where this client lived, when they pulled him over. So, the police had their story thinking he was going to threaten the person, and he got 5 years. In my eyes he was a good bloke, who wouldn't hurt a fly. He's a top man and a good friend.

X-factor was on TV and everyone was watching it, and Honey G was on there. Everybody loved her because she was so shit. When she came on, everybody started banging their cell doors and going mad saying, 'We're on lockdown,' the way she says. Everybody was screaming, 'H/to the/O to the/N to the/E to the/Y…HONEY G!' I wondered if everybody was smoking crack in here, as it was so hilarious.

I had a letter from Heather Howe saying Merry Christmas, keep your head up high. I was grateful for that, and thought it was nice of her to send me a card, and the bonus was that it had some great news inside. I was finally back up in court in the new year, on the 6th of January. The letter said, 'If you plead guilty to conspiracy of weed, they will drop the conspiracy supply of the Cocaine.'

I thought, so they bloody should, as I didn't have anything to do with it. It was such a relief, knowing this was going to be dropped, as it is a very bad thing to have on your name. So, I rang Heather and asked her how long she thought I would get for involvement in the sale of the weed.

She told me that they couldn't get an accurate number on how much weed was sold, or how many kilos there were, so they were going to estimate. She turned around and said that I was looking at a possible 3 years and a maximum of 5 years for my involvement. Even 3 years I thought was fucking high as I was only the person picking the money up. Nothing more, nothing less.

Still, I was relieved now things were moving, as now I had my court date set. Surely they would see in court that my role in this wasn't so bad, and I was praying and wishing that they would. I was hoping for a reasonable sentence, or even freedom, with my time spent already.

It was New Year's Eve, and I'd had the shittiest Xmas ever. I was so stressed out over all this involvement in the case, and to make things worse, I'd had tickets booked ages back for another holiday in Thailand this Xmas, and I was missing out on that, as I was stuck in this shit-hole awaiting my fate.

CHAPTER THIRTY-THREE

The 6th of January had arrived, and I was taken to the courts. I was nervous, but in high spirits, and just wanted it over and done with.

I was told that the judge who was taking this case on, had it in for the main person in this case, and anybody who runs or mixes with him, but I didn't think much of this, as I hadn't had much to do with the main person. As a matter of fact, I didn't even know my co-defendants, so I thought all of this wouldn't affect me. I had lived in Spain for so long, so nobody really knew much about me, including the police and the courts. They did drop the conspiracy A Cocaine, but I wasn't really that relieved about it, as I knew I had fuck all to do with it, and I was not guilty, but in the back of my mind I was happy.

Then the judge started talking and said he could not be sure on how much weed was supplied, and I didn't really know either. As I kept on telling them, I was just supposed to pick money up and that was it. Then, to my shock and horror, he referred to me as leading role, which means I'm the head person, but I wasn't, I was less role. Just the driver. That's all.

The judge had estimated that there was up to one hundred, and maybe up to a ton supplied. I was like, 'You're mad.' Then, I realised what the other co-defendants had said. They were right. He had it in for anyone on this case, but this was not sufficient evidence, nothing but hearsay. He left the courtroom.

He returned after thirty minutes. He took in my early plea of guilty for the weed, but then he said 'I'm not giving you the full thirty three percent off, as you were on the run in Spain.'

I said, 'Judge, this is a joke. I have lived in Spain for 16 years; I didn't run there.'

He told me to be quiet, and said 'I'm giving you now twenty five percent because of it.' Then he said, 'For this crime…'

And it went silent, and I couldn't wait for him to say something. I was hoping he would turn around and say, 'with all you've been through already, I'm giving you a suspended sentence.' I was really hoping for this and praying.

The pause was like a lifetime. Then, he started to talk. He said, 'I'm starting this sentence at ten years, and with your twenty five percent off, I'm sentencing you to seven and a half years inside.'

I just couldn't believe it. Was I really hearing this? I just felt this massive blow as if someone had just kicked me in the balls, or did someone just pull my pants down, and fuck me in the arse. Well, they might as well have. I didn't think my body could hold itself up. I went light and felt giddy as though all my power had been sucked from me, and I was about to hit the floor.

Then, he said there was more. I thought, oh my God, what's he going on about? Does he think he's fucking Oliver Twist? More?

He turned around and said, 'We are preparing your papers for P.O.C.A.' At the time I didn't really understand what this meant, but my lawyer later told me this is the Proceeds of Crime Act. I told my lawyer I didn't earn much out of this A couple of grand and that was it. And to be honest, they can fucking have it back! Look at the mess it's got me into.

Well, that was it, I was sentenced. I just couldn't quite believe it. Over the next few days after this, I was so quiet, as I was in shock.

Everybody couldn't believe it. People were starting to get worried about me too, as I was so quiet. I just walked around like the rest of the zombies. I might as well have smoked the spice myself. I just wasn't me anymore. As far as I was concerned, the good LOTD, the loving, funny, caring person had died in me, and I had become a zombie.

After that court case, Heather got back in touch with me, and explained the sentence was far too heavy. She said that she had already filed an appeal on my behalf, but to be honest I'd lost all hope. Everything she said went in one ear and out the other, and I was in a zombie state. All I could think about was the massive sentence I'd been given. I thought to myself, happy New Year LOTD. Not!

Weeks had passed now, and Heather had been back in contact, and told me that the appeal had been sent off. She told me she was waiting to hear back from them. I still wasn't right, but then again who would be. Also, I was starting to get pissed off on B wing. I needed a change, as I'd just got my enhanced status. I wanted to end being in the madness of this wing.

I arrived on the F2 enhanced wing, and I was buzzing. Everybody tries to get onto F2, because it's quieter, and there is a toaster and a microwave, and an outside yard. Also, you are allowed out of your cell until 7pm every night. I was happier about the situation I was in. This was where I met one of my best buddies, Simon Gray, and many others, Phil, Paul, Trevor, and Tyson.

One day I was talking with my best buddy Si, and he worked as a red band, which means you can move around the prison quite easily. He was working for the inside national career service, and he drops mail off to all the other wings in the prison. The part of his job he hated was that he had to drop the mail into E wing, which is the sex-offenders wing.

While he was there, he spotted this bloke they call Emma. Obviously, he is a transvestite. He or she came out of their cell in full makeup, and hair in bunches, and shouted out to all the other inmates on the wing, 'Right, who's been in my cell and nicked my baccy? If it's not back in my cell within twenty minutes, I'm going to grass you lot up, and name those who I give blow jobs to.'

Well, my mate Simon was in stitches. As he was just about to leave E wing, he passed Emma's cell, and said, 'Emma, did you get your baccy back?'

She replied, 'Yes, I think the last comment got it back!' As Simon told me, I was pissing myself with laughter too.

I settled onto F2 nicely, and bought myself a PlayStation, stereo and a DVD player, to help the time go by. Two of my best friends were coming to visit me from the outside. It was Pete and Norm, and it was lovely to see them, and it was a great visit.

Also, my family came to see me on my birthday, and it was the first time I'd seen my new granddaughter. Wow, she is so beautiful, such a lovely little girl. I'm so proud. I was so happy, and it made my day, also with Mini Me being there too. My new little granddaughter is mixed race. She's half English and half Jamaican, and she sure is a stunner. Well, I've never been to Jamaica before, so when I'm out I'm looking forward to going over and meeting some of my distant relatives.

As you can see, I was trying my best to do my time, and make the time go as quickly as possible. My appeal was coming up soon, and I couldn't wait for this day, and I received the go-ahead. It was agreed that I had good grounds to appeal my sentence. So, you can imagine I was totally buzzing. As you know, they gave me far too long for my part in this case. It was a joke.

While inside I had to enrol on some courses, as part of my sentence plan, and it's called the Sycamore Tree, and it was nothing I had ever come across in my life before. It's a life victim awareness programme on the impact of crime, taking responsibility, awareness of victims, showing remorse, saying sorry. And real people come in to talk about what happened to them. These people were real victims. I did other courses too, the Get it Right programme, and I completed the Samaritans course, and became a Listener, to help other inmates out.

The date had come for my appeal. I did it by video link, as I didn't want to go to London, to either Brixton or Pentonville prison for it, as I would have lost my cell on the F2 enhanced wing.

The appeal court is the Royal Appeal High Court at the Strand in London, and my appeal went up in front of three judges. A screw called me into the room where the video link was. I waited for the three judges to come into the courtroom, and we were all told to sit down.

My barrister did lots of talking. Some made some sense, some didn't. It all went very quick. The three judges left the room, and were back within fifteen minutes, with the new verdict.

I was told to rise by the centre judge, and he said, 'We have taken it all in, and we are reducing your sentence, from seven and a half years, to a new five years, four months.'

At first, I was happy, then I thought it still wasn't enough. So, there I was after my appeal with mixed feelings. Of course, I was happy, as I'd had my sentence reduced, but I still felt given the part I played in this case, it was still not enough. In these situations, you just have to bite the bullet, and get on with it.

CHAPTER THIRTY-FOUR

While I was in prison - I'm not going to go all deeply religious on you or spooky, but as a kid I've always prayed, and prayed throughout my life, but I never went to church before. But now I was going, as these were dark parts of my life, and I found refuge in the church, and learned more about Jesus Christ and the study of The Bible.

This is where I found myself and started to believe, and even from the first day I went to church, I left with a warmth and a smile on my face. I felt loved and cared for. It gave me a boost of energy and made me think, with a little bit of my normal self coming back. The church made me see the light and the future. The church helped me so much. The volunteers that came to the prison were amazing people, giving up their free time for this, to help people in need.

I completed a course at church called the Alpha course, which I'm ever so proud about. Still to this day, the church is a big part of my life.

Well, time was going, but it defo wasn't like the saying when time flies, because it doesn't in prison. If anybody says it does, they need their head checking. My sentence was down to one year and eight months, when a screw knocked on my door saying, 'Wrighty, get your stuff, you're being transferred to Stocken.'

This is a C cat prison and is up in Leicestershire somewhere, and I thought, here we go again. It was a three-hour prison van trip up there, and an absolute nightmare. You're looking out of the window at the normal day, and life going about its business, and you wish you were out there doing the same.

While in the van, I wrote this poem.

> One of the good things about prison is detox
> You're not contaminated with any
> Alcohol or drugs and your mind is
> So clear and focused and you think about your life
> Where you went right and where you went wrong
> And I do regret some of the things I have done in my life
> But there is some I don't
>
> I think in life I didn't want it to be easy
> The harder the better as it makes you push for it
> I didn't want the nine to five
> I didn't want routine
> Maybe stable is not for me
> I don't want things on a plate
> Maybe I wanted to be difficult
> Plain is not for me
>
> If I had an easy life it wouldn't be a challenge
> I like different
> As mad as it sounds, I like problems
> If not, it would be too easy
> If I did hurt people, well I am sorry
> And if I made you smile and laugh then I am happy
> But whatever I did in life is life

I arrived in Stocken. I met some great mates here. There was Gary, who is nicknamed big G, and he was from Sutton. There was Kingy from Nottingham, Anthony from Mansfield, and there was Doncaster Mick, and Lee Kendall from Brighton. I became very good friends with them. I met another bloke called Stuart. He was put in prison for handling jewellery from the Hatton Garden heist. These were all top people.

I met this one lad in here, and he was in for dangerous driving, and he was telling me what happened. I just couldn't quite believe it when he told me about it. His wife was about to give birth to their second child. With the first child his wife had problems and she nearly lost her life, so they weren't taking any chances.

They rang for an ambulance, but the operator said that there was none available, so they rang the hospital, and the hospital knew about the previous problems, so they advised him to drive as quickly as possible to the hospital. So, he got his wife into the car and headed straight for the hospital. He didn't know on this particular day that a woman unknown to him was signing herself out of the hospital. She was a self-harmer who had tried to kill herself on many occasions. That was why she was at the hospital that day as she had made yet another attempt to end her life.

Anyway, they were getting closer and closer to the hospital. His wife was screaming in pain in the back of the car, and he was doing his best to get there in these circumstances. They were coming to the hospital entrance, with him checking and looking in the mirror, making sure his wife was okay. He didn't realise or notice that the lady who had signed herself out of the hospital had come outside the entrance. He just didn't see her as he looked in the mirror to check his wife. He didn't expect a lady to be lying in the middle of the road, and he ran over her. Well, you can imagine what happened. She died.

He did get his wife into the hospital thankfully, and she gave birth to their son, and they were all okay, but he and his wife were in bits with shock, and so upset about what had happened to the lady. But the police and the courts still put him away for dangerous driving, and he got a three-year sentence. I will leave my comment out of this, for you to decide on your own.

Time was moving but not going fast enough for me. Some weeks and days I felt so low and down, and some were better than others, but you just try to make the most of things inside and use your time. Sometimes it's not the things going on inside the prison. It's the problems going on outside the prison that get to you more, because you're stuck in there and you can do fuck all about it. Some of the things outside the prison were breaking me. Some of my so-called friends and even family that you really thought would help you in these times, didn't. They just took the piss, because they know you could do fuck all about it. But believe you me, I thought, when I get out, there will be words and my thoughts to say about this.

Me and my pal Lee, nicknamed Goldfingers, entered a pool competition on the wing. There were sixteen players in all, and everybody put a pound item in from the canteen. Me and Lee said we'd split it if we ended up in the final, which we both did, but fair play, Lee did beat me. Hence his nickname Goldfingers. I'd still won though, because we split the prizes. It was a top weekend, that pool competition.

There was another young lad on the wing called Tommy. He was a big lad with tattoos of tears under his eyes. I got on really well with him, but he was always off his face on something. Then, there was another lad on the wing. They thought he was a grass. Whether he was or not, nobody knew. Maybe it was just the look of his face. I think Tommy stuck a china mug right in his face. There was claret everywhere. The bloke was lucky not to lose one of his eyes. Big Tommy got sent down the block and was sent back to B cat prison status. He would get an extra two to three years for this, if not more. He got in at 19 years old and was 26 at the time. He had pulled a makeshift knife out on an officer as well. Is this lad ever going to get out of prison?

I remember another time playing pool with this little Rastafarian. He was a great pool player, and whenever he won the game, he would look at you with his eyes, and close his eyelids, and the mad fucker had tattooed on one eyelid, *game* and on the other it said *over*! Everyone thought how totally mad it was.

This bloke was a great craftsman too. He used to collect the bars of soap and carve shapes and objects out of them. He showed me one of his carvings, which was a boat. He had so much talent, but he also had major drug problems.

He had other carvings too. He had made a gun and the bullets to go with it. It was just so wicked and real, and he was so proud of it too, and so would I be. But one day the screws spun his cell as they thought he had drugs in there. They never found any but what they did find was the soap gun and the bullets. They confiscated them, saying they needed to be destroyed as they were a symbol of gang crime, and would not be tolerated in the prison.

Then one day to his surprise, he was getting a bollocking for keeping his music on too loud in his cell, so he was sent down to see the S.O. in his office. To his disbelief when he got there, he noticed the S.O. had kept his soap gun and bullets on his mantelpiece. He couldn't believe it. As you can guess it's okay for some, but not for others!

One day I had my prison canteen list come through, under my door as normal, and there was this little computer pocket game you could buy. It had all the old favourites, Pac Man, Astro Wars, Donkey Kong, and many more. It was a great little game to help time go by. Well, you are not going to believe what happened next.

I was in bed one night, and I was playing my little game, with my lights off in my cell. It was letting off a little light. The night screw came round for his checks, and when he got to my cell, he looked through the panel at me, so I put my thumb up, and showed him the sign that I was fine, and carried on playing my game, but he didn't fuck off. He just kept staring at me. Then he left but he returned five minutes later. I was still playing my game, and he stared again, so I just shouted to him, 'Fuck off, you bloody weirdo,' and carried on playing my game.

First thing the next morning, I woke up to the cell door coming in, with three big screws, shouting, 'Where's the phone, Wrighty?'

I was like, 'What the fuck are you going on about?' Then it all came to me. It must have been the night screw, him thinking I had a phone. So, I showed them my pocket game, and said it must have been this, while the screws all just started laughing and left me to it.

Then I thought to myself, I wouldn't just be lying there, texting on my phone, and telling him to fuck off, would I? But I was glad that was the end of that, as it was a serious nicking that could have led to two years extra inside prison.

Here in HMP Stocken, like in HMP Bullingdon, there are major drug problems - drugs like spice, and also a drug called Subutex. This is in a tablet form but once crushed up they snort it, throwing up the nostrils which is supposed to give you a massive high which is very dangerous and highly addictive. Many people become hooked on it.

Most of the drugs that come into the prison, if you can believe it come through the prison post. There is not enough man power too physically check it all. Other places are the visitor halls as family members and friends past it on there. I've heard mums doing it. I even heard this one time they used their own baby! They put drugs in the nappy!

It's terrible but they will do anything to get things inside the prison walls. It is also true that they are using drones from outside to fly things up to inmates' windows. Drop offs can be anything from KFC to Mac Donald's, to more dangerous stuff like drugs, weapons, and mobile phones. Mobile phones can command up to a thousand pounds for smart phones. There is the prison favourite mobile. It's a small phone called the mars bar. It's the size of your big finger, so it's easy for the inmate to hide with them inserting it up the anal, so it's never ever found by the screws.

There are other ways to get things inside the prison walls too. They get thrown over the walls at certain times, knowing that the inmates are on garden duty, so they can receive them and pass them on around the prison. At the start of the sentence before being sent down, some load themselves up, either by swallowing or insert packages up their anal. Drugs go for big prices in prisons and some inmates are making a lot of money and get sent into prison just for this. It's that mad!

There are just so many ways to get contrabands into the prison that the prison staff find it more or less impossible to stop it. It's getting out of control and is causing a massive strain on the prison system. Prison healthcare too is coming to breaking point, as they are constantly dealing with overdosing, and the self-harmers and peoples' mental health care.

There are so many inmates with mental health problems. There was this one young lad having been in quite a few years and he'd given himself a Chelsea smile both sides of his mouth, which he will have to live with for the rest of he's life. It's so sad. There are many others that do damage to their arms and legs. Some of these people are in terrible state. It's awful. Even to see all this puts your own head into mental state. There was this other young lad in Bullingdon who was hanging from the light with bed sheets. We had to cut him down. Lucky for him, he's still alive.

Then there was this other bloke called Evans. He had crazy mental health issues. He actually thought he was going out with Kate Slater in EastEnders, and whenever the program was on TV, without fail he would be glued to it. Whenever the character Kate Slater kissed someone else, he would scream at the top of his voice, 'Kate Slater, you slag!' And then he would start smashing his cell up, and kicking his cell door.

He also had a thing for Lousie Rednapp. One of the other inmates wrote him a letter pretending to be her, and put it under his cell door like the prison mail. Over the next few months, it was all he would go on about, that she had written to him. It's sad really, but some people think it's funny. But these people with mental problems need help, not other people messing them up more.

I heard about one inmate with mental health problems smoking too much spice, and he cut his own cock off. That's terrible. Some of the prison wings are like the movie Shutter Island.

Another way of making money in the prison system was to set up your own shop, either selling food, or baccy, or smoking capsules. The seller would give you what you want on tick until Friday when everyone got their canteen, but if you didn't pay up, then you had to return the items back double or even in some cases treble. And if you didn't do that, you were in big trouble. They called it black eye Friday at Stocken, as that's when, if u don't pay the shop back, you get a kicking and the following week they double it up again and again. The people that don't pay up and get smashed up get moved off the wing to another one for their own protection. But people have friends in all the prison wings so this can be a very dangerous thing too. In my opinion just don't borrow. Only spend what you can and get on with it.

Stocken had a good library which I used, and I went to church there too, and became part of the prison band. On a Sunday everyone would come down to the church and see the band. I was head singer and I got called Oasis which I though was hilarious. We really did have some top days out down at the church there. It always gave me a great feeling after singing. It made me feel alive again, and that I wasn't inside the prison walls. On returning back to my cell though that feeling would soon leave me, I was back in prison again.

My best friend Lee, Goldfingers, got his D cat so it was sad to see him go. But I was still here with Gary and Tony, and we would play Tiger Woods on the Play Station 2 most days. We had a great laugh together, and it made the time go so much quicker. Gary had the biggest stash of porn mags on the wing too, and it did make me laugh to see people cue up at his cell door before lockup to grab the Razzel.

My time in Stocken was coming to an end as I was being sent back too Bullingdon for my P.O.C.A. Over the next few weeks I just got my head down and got on with time. My court date was coming up soon back down in Oxford so I knew I'd be transferred back down to Bullingdon. But things suddenly started to get difficult with my health. I was getting chest pains, with my heart beating all over the place and a pain in my left armpit. My left hand had pins and needles. I was sweating, and I didn't feel at all well.

They rushed me down to healthcare and put me on an ECG machine. I spent most of the day there. I met a lovely nurse named Crystal. During my stay at healthcare, there was a spice attack. In this week two people had died in the prison from spice attacks, as there was a bad batch going around. Also, to my disbelief, this man came into healthcare, with a deodorant roll stuck up his arse. He was obviously gay, and playing about with himself, and it got stuck up there, and went sideways inside him. They had to take him to the hospital to get it removed.

Later that evening, I had calmed down, and they sent me back to my cell, and told the night screw to keep an eye on me. They put it all down to stress with the P.O.C.A.

CHAPTER THIRTY-FIVE

The day had come for me to leave Stocken, and I was back in the van. As we were passing back down towards Oxfordshire, we had to drop another inmate to Luton Crown Court. As we drove into the area, I had floods of memories. My mum had lived in Luton, and I felt really sad.

Finally, we arrived back at Bullingdon. They put me back on the toxic F1 starters wing. I spoke to S.O. Blackford. He said there was no room on the cosier F2 wing for now, but he got me a single cell on C wing, which I appreciated. I met a good friend here, called Millwall Mark, and we reminisced about old football days. There was another bloke here called Trevor, but he wasn't very clever. This was the third time I'd seen him come in and out of prison during on my own sentence.

After a few days, I arrived back on the cosier wing of F2. It had changed loads. Most of my friends had gone, including my best buddy Simon, but my other good friend Trevor was still there. What was so strange was I only ended up in my old mate Simon's cell! It just felt mad, as I knew what he went through in this cell, as his brother died on the outside. He had committed suicide. While lying on the bed one day, I could actually feel Simon's pain and suffering. It was so weird to sense his feelings of such emotional sadness. Then, two days later, I myself was found lying on the floor. The next minute, I was being flashed through traffic in an ambulance, heading towards the hospital.

Yet again, I was having a massive panic attack. My chest felt as though it was being crushed, and my heart was beating like the drums in the track by Phil Collins *In The Air Tonight,* but without the air. I was in a terrible state. I thought I was having a massive heart attack.

Luckily for me the next day, after spending such a night, I was alive. I wasn't one hundred percent, but they returned me to prison anyway.

I was still attending my Sunday Christian service at church, and also on a Wednesday. I would attend the Alpha course too, where I met a sweet, lovely lady, called Susan. She was from America, and I told her about my mum, with that telephone call I missed, and how much it was affecting me that I didn't say goodbye.

As I've said, I'm not totally religious, but she said we could reach out for her. I said yes, so together we sat on the floor, with Susan talking, and us both praying. That's when I felt a presence. It felt as if my mum was actually there. It was a warm feeling, but it gave me goose bumps. It was an experience I'd never felt before.

I started to talk with my mum, apologising to her about the missed call and all the shit that I'd got involved in. It was just amazing to have this happen. I still can't quite believe it now, but it happened, which gave me such joy to finally have said our goodbyes.

Getting back to my P.O.C.A - this is money the police want when they think you have made it from a crime, but in my case, I made hardly fuck all. It was stressful enough to try and find the money, but if you don't, you end up doing more time. Luckily for me I had good friends, and it was paid, and the extra time for it wasn't added to my sentence. That was a massive weight off my shoulders, which made me very happy. And my family.

Well, apparently not all my family. A mutual friend of ours rang my brother to tell him the good news, that I no longer had to do the extra time inside. He was playing golf at the time of the phone call, and he complained that the phone call had ruined his day, and his round of golf, before he put the phone down. Thanks bro, but no thanks.

With my P.O.C.A. paid, I was finally being moved to D cat open prison, and this was another step towards freedom.

I was on a high. At last, with my final steps towards freedom, I was buzzing big time. I just could not wait to get there, as life to me would be coming back finally. It made me quite emotional.

I knew I was going to be reunited with Lee too. My friend Goldfingers! I hadn't seen him for quite a while now since he left Stocken, and it would make my day to meet up with him again.

CHAPTER THIRTY-SIX

My arrival at HMP Ford felt amazing. No more bolts or bars, high fences, or doors being locked. It had been some time since I felt like this, and it truly felt like real life again.

HMP Ford is an old RAF base. It opened up as a prison in 1961, and it still houses prisoners in the old billets that the pilots used to sleep in. The place was quite rundown, like most of the UK prisons, but one thing was good, I was half free. Like one foot in the door, and one foot out the door. That was the feeling I got. You could do loads of exercise here. If you walked around the entire place, twelve laps, it was the equivalent of eight miles.

At first you had to go in the billets, to double up. After that you went to the brick building single rooms. On my billet I ended up meeting some good friends. There was big Bob from London, kickboxer Paul from Aldershot. Now Paul was a hard man. He would just eat up the twelve laps round the base for breakfast, and then do another twelve at night. He was fit as a fiddle. He used to cut my hair too, doing a fantastic job. We did have some laughs me and him, and we're still in touch today, with me being invited to all his fights.

There was another bloke called Paddy, and a bloke called Panama. I couldn't believe it, but he lived in Panama and we had been drinking in the same bars in the city. And finally, I got to be reunited with Lee Goldfingers. We found it overwhelming to see each other again.

I met another bloke here, called Big Sleepy John. It didn't matter where you were with him. Eating, or in the library, or in the church, he would just fall asleep. It did make me laugh.

I met another bloke called big Paul, top guy and we became close friends. There was this one night me and him were walking around the grounds, then five big black bags came flying over the perimeter fence, with SAS style inmates dressed in black, receiving them. It did crack us both up, and it was exciting to watch.

With this being a D cat, you could get outside work, and have day release from the prison, and weekends away back home. Well, there was this one day I was out on day release, and I missed my stop. I only bloody ended up in Haslemere, which was fucking miles away. I nearly didn't get the train back in time, but I got to the gate by the skin of my teeth.

At Ford I met these four old guys, who were called the Jersey four. I became quite close to one of them. Well, he told me the story. They had bought a load of hash in France and were smuggling it into Jersey, as the price there is ten times much more. Anyway, they had three in a boat, and they were coming to the shores of Jersey at night-time to smuggle it in under darkness, with one of them sitting in the jeep onshore, waiting for them, but the satnav they had on the boat had packed up, and they nearly went to the wrong island, the neighbouring island of Guernsey. They finally got back on course to Jersey, but now they were panicking as the boat was taking on water. Also without their knowledge, some fucker had stitched them up and the police were waiting for them. The one that was waiting in the jeep for them to come ashore had fallen asleep.

When the boat finally made it ashore, the police nicked all three of them. On the way back to the police vans, they noticed an old guy in a jeep with his head down, so the police knocked on the window and asked what he was doing there, and if he was okay. He only turned around and said that he was waiting for those three!

Time went a lot quicker in D cat, and it helped me a lot before my release, as I was a broken man from what I had been through. The open prison helped prepare me for the great world outside.

I had a week to go, and I just couldn't quite believe it. A fresh start. A new life. New chapters. And my daughter had just given birth to my adorable grandson. I was well made up, and I would become good friends of the other grandad Marlon.

The week had gone, and that was it, I was at the gate. It was my release date. There's nothing in the world like having the feeling you are free. FREEDOM! I was very emotional with joy, and I did shed some tears, not sad ones, happy ones, with flashes of my journey in getting here.

It was tough, but I was proud of myself, that I had survived it, but let's get it right, there was many times I did break. But now it was my freedom. I shouted out loud, 'COME ON!' as I finally left the gates behind me. 'COME ON LOTD.'

LIFE AFTER

Two weeks after leaving prison, I found out both of my dogs had passed away. I've had to rebuild my life as I lost everything with having to get a new home. I also have been having bad problems with my disability, and I have had to be seen by a mental health team

I have been having great moments with my kids and grandkids, and I have set up on the South coast to start to rebuild my life.

Most of all I would like to make this point very clear.

STAY AWAY FROM DRUGS.

Drugs will ruin your life and others.

Take no part in them either. Look where it got me.

I no longer take drugs myself and I have no involvement with them or anyone to do with them.

Since not taking drugs my life feels much more real, and my life is much happier.

I really believe all this and I now help others with such problems and helping them to rehabilitation.

And I now follow the path of God, being a Christian.

Thank you all for taking your time with me and joining me on my journey.
LOTD
Lloyd Wright

Lightning Source UK Ltd.
Milton Keynes UK
UKHW020242231121
394401UK00006B/129

9 781800 312210